THE JOYRIDE

By
Joy Mormur

Enjoy the ride!
Joy

IPG
Intermedia Publishing Group

THE JOYRIDE

Published by:
Intermedia Publishing Group, Inc.
P.O. Box 2825
Peoria, Arizona 85380
www.intermediapub.com

ISBN 978-1-935529-74-3

Printed in the United States of America

INTRODUCTION

Have you ever become so discouraged with the daily grind of life that you felt like just taking off with no destination in mind? After six years of struggling as a single mother, Joy Mormur fulfills a life long dream of traveling around the United States on *Bessie*, her Harley-Davidson motorcycle. But her trip was more than just an adventurous trek across America-it was a search for answers. Follow Joy through her tales of the eight months, 19,000 miles, twenty-three states journey. Find out how she was transformed from a broken-hearted woman into the "Joy" she had been searching for.

TABLE OF CONTENTS

This book is dedicated to all bikers.

This is a true story.
Occasionally names have been altered to
protect the privacy of individuals involved.

CHAPTER 1
LET YOUR DREAMS TAKE FLIGHT

Psalm 34:18
The Lord is close to the brokenhearted and saves those who are crushed in spirit.

"You're going alone?" my friends asked me in shock. "You're going to travel around the United States for a year on your Harley and stay in campgrounds all by yourself?"

"Yes," I replied, "I'm going alone." ALONE! I had always hated that word and I hated living alone. But here I was once again—alone at thirty-six years of age. All I had ever wanted from life was a happy marriage with a lifelong companion to share the joys and struggles of everyday life. But the one thing I so desperately desired had eluded me.

One of the times I don't mind being alone, though, is when I hop on *Bessie,* my Harley-Davidson motorcycle, and take her for a ride. She is six hundred pounds of vibrating chrome and steel between my legs. When I open her throttle, I feel powerful and in control. As I wind her down the road my problems and cares seem to blow behind me into the wind. With the sun shining on my face, I feel happy and free—and

I'm alone! Well, not totally alone because wherever I go, God is with me.

We've had quite a few conversations on my rides. The only problem is that although I consider my relationship with God to be the most important relationship in my life, it's not enough: I can't feel Him wrap His arms around me, I can't see Him look into my eyes, and I can't smell Him. I always felt a little guilty about God not being enough until I read in the Bible that even though God walked and talked with Adam in the Garden of Eden, He saw that Adam needed a *human* companion. So he created Eve. Even after all the pain and rejection I had experienced from past relationships, I never gave up on finding my "Adam," the companion God created for me. However, that bottomless black pit of loneliness drove me into my self-destructive habits. To help me through those dark times, I got involved in counseling, twelve-step meetings, and in church. Although these avenues have helped me grow, it always seemed for every three steps forward, I took two steps back. But as my sister, Charen, pointed out to me—at least I'm still one step ahead! And as my twelve-step friends reminded me—it's progress not perfection.

One lonely night about a month before I left on my trip, I lay in bed wrapped around my pillow, and cried out to God, "I hate being alone. I want so much to have a husband to love me. Okay God, I accept I'm alone. I'm ready to learn what I'm supposed to by being alone. It's just you and me God—find me a husband quick!" You can see that I bounced between acceptance and panic!

I did have a husband once. When I was seventeen, we ran off together to pursue this romantic dream of traveling around the United States on his motorcycle. But we had problems from the beginning. We lived in Illinois and his bike had been stored with a friend who lived in Georgia. By the time we arrived in Georgia, with only $200 in our pockets, we discovered that his so-called friend had disappeared. All that was left of our dream was a steel frame—the bike had been stripped and all the parts had been sold. So we rented a mobile home while we both went to work to save enough money for the trip back home to Illinois.

During our short stay in Georgia I learned how to ride a motorcycle. Our next-door neighbor had his 90cc Yamaha dirt bike out one day riding it around his front yard. I ran over and asked if he would teach me how to ride. It was such a little bike, I thought, what could be so hard about riding it? He let me climb on and I asked, "How do you do it?"

My neighbor replied, "Open the clutch slowly and at the same time give it gas." That sounded easy enough. As soon as I tried to follow his instructions, the bike pulled right out from under me. The only way I could hold on was to run behind it. I suddenly realized that I had forgotten to ask how to stop it! So I let go of the bike and watched helplessly as it crashed into my neighbor's trailer. This was definitely not the safest way to learn how to ride a bike! Fortunately, the only damage done was a small dent in my neighbor's trailer, so he picked up the bike and brought it back over to me. After receiving a few more directions, I tried it again. By that afternoon, I felt confident enough to venture out onto the fire trails in the woods behind our trailers. I was hooked on riding!

After a couple months, my husband and I had saved enough money to go back home. However, the rest of our marriage continued to be a string of disappointments. I became locked in a cycle of abuse, broken promises, and shattered dreams. After thirteen years of struggling, I finally broke free from my destructive marriage.

I found myself alone and lonely with the responsibility of raising two children. Pursuing my love of motorcycles, however, seemed a good way to meet people and occupy my spare time. But this time I took a beginners motorcycle rider course offered by the Motorcycle Safety Foundation. My fear that I'd be the only woman in the class was soon forgotten when I discovered that the instructor was a woman! Upon completion of the course, I proudly received my motorcycle driver's license. The 650cc Yamaha I bought for $200 was down more than running, so I affectionately named it my *Yamabomber.* It took me two more years just to save for the down payment on my dream bike—a Harley-Davidson.

Fortunately, I was living in Daytona Beach at the time, a biker's paradise and host to the world renowned Bike Week since 1937. Those ten days were the most exhilarating time of year for me as Daytona Beach was taken over by several hundred thousand bikers from all over the world. Anywhere I went Bike Week; I could hear the roaring thunder of Harley-Davidson's that filled the air with their beckoning call. The low deep throttle of those machines aroused a longing in me for the freedom of the open road.

The best place to admire those beasts was on Main Street where hundreds of Harleys lined up for blocks on both sides of the road. I spent many nights walking up and down Main Street absorbing the electric charged atmosphere as thousands of chrome polished Harleys with their black leather clad riders continuously paraded up and down the street. Being in their midst fueled my dreams as much as wind fans an open field fire.

My favorite place to go Bike Week was the Harley-Davidson demo tent where I got to test-drive any model Harley I wanted. My dream was a step closer to reality—I didn't own a Harley yet but I knew I could ride one! An important aspect of my dream was that it was something I could do by myself. Although I preferred to share it with someone, I didn't want my dream to depend on anyone else but me. That way no one could take it away from, let me down, or disappoint me.

My non-stop talking about my dream to my co-workers probably drove them crazy! In fact, one night as I was fantasizing about how much fun it would be to travel around the United States for a whole year on a Harley, write a book about the adventure, then try to get on Johnny Carson's *The Tonight Show*, a co-worker replied, "You'll never do it." Her absolute negativity both shocked and silenced me, but I secretly vowed nothing would stop me from making my dream a reality. Surprisingly, this same woman later gave me a poster with a picture of Pegasus (which I have tattooed on my abdomen) with the caption, "Let Your Dreams Take Flight."

Meanwhile, my sister Charen had given me the name and phone number for the president of the Christian Motorcyclists Association of Daytona Beach and suggested I call for information on events. She thought that if I met Christian bikers they could help me find what I was so desperately missing. Although I felt terribly shy reaching out to total strangers, I gave the president a call and found out a memorial parade was scheduled that weekend in honor of a policeman who had been killed in Daytona Beach. The president told me I could meet the club members at the event. The idea of riding with hundreds of Harley riders on my *Yamabomber* terrified me. I asked him if he knew someone who would ride over with me. He gave me the phone number of a woman who was a member of the Tribe of Judah Motorcycle Ministries. Feeling grateful that I was going to meet another woman rider, I gave her a call and we set up a time and place to meet. I'll never forget the day I pulled into the parking lot where we were meeting. My brakes as usual squealed loudly. My new friend cracked up laughing and exclaimed, "Boy, are you going to get teased riding that!" Her welcome did not help ease my fears any. But I felt a little better when I saw that she wasn't riding a Harley-Davidson either. Little did I know that this meeting was the beginning of a long friendship.

I started reading biker magazines to learn as much as I could about the sport of motorcycling. One day I saw an ad for a book called *On the Perimeter*, the autobiography of Hazel Kolb a.k.a. "Motorcyclin' Gran'ma." After receiving the book, I couldn't stop reading. Hazel Kolb was an inspiration to my dream, but also a shocking disappointment. She had already lived my dream, written a book about it, and even appeared on Johnny Carson's *The Tonight Show*! Well, I guess you can't be first at everything, but for me, my trip, which I affectionately named *The Joyride,* would be my first dream to come true. So I continued to work toward my goal.

After two more years I had saved enough money for the down payment on my dream bike that I had chosen during my demo rides. Although I preferred the style of some of the other models of Harley, I decided on a 1991 FXRS Low Rider Convertible because it has a rubber-mounted engine, which makes for a very smooth ride. This factor would be more important for comfort when I embarked on my long trip around the United States than how my bike looked. Also, the bike came equipped with a windshield and saddlebags.

I enrolled in the Motorcycle Safety Foundation's "Better Biker Class" to help familiarize myself with my new motorcycle *Bessie,* which I named in honor of my grandmother. She had been my favorite lady in the whole world and I really missed her after she passed away. My Aunt Frances, Bessie's daughter, told me that when she was a teenager, Bessie had warned her to stay away from "those awful bikers and to never get on a motorcycle." Imagine Grandma Bessie's surprise if she knew that today her granddaughter now rides a motorcycle named after her! Of course, the image of bikers has drastically changed through the years and all kinds of people ride all different types of motorcycles.

After three more years of hard work, I had enough money to make the rest of my dream a reality. However, I became very fearful. Even though *The Joyride* was something I knew I could do alone, in the back of my mind I really had pictured riding off into the sunset with a man. But I was still single and alone. On top of that, after three years of sobriety, I was now nine months into a relapse of smoking pot and drinking. The only thing that seemed to be going right was my career. As a supervisor for a private laboratory, I really liked my job and my co-workers, and the salary and hours couldn't be beat. Should I give up the security of my job and leave everything and everyone behind?

Originally, I had planned on attempting *The Joyride* several years later. Because I had been so depressed, perhaps I was merely running away. After spending a weekend contemplating and agonizing about my decision, I concluded that this was not only the right time to go but it was literally what I needed to do to save my life. Even though I was about to fulfill a lifelong dream, I still felt paralyzed with fear. But I reminded myself that courage was feeling the fear and doing it anyway! The following Monday morning I handed in my resignation.

CHAPTER 2
THE SURPRISE BEGINNING!

Psalm 37:4
Delight yourself in the Lord and he will give you the desires of your heart.

After handing in my resignation letter, I had thirty days to ready myself for the trip as I planned on leaving by the end of October 1993. Already experienced at packing for short trips, I had a pretty good idea of what I needed. A tent that would fit on my motorcycle was the only item I had to purchase. I wanted a large tent, at least one I could stand up in, in case adverse weather kept me tent bound. And of course I had to be able to put up the tent by myself. I chose a nine by twelve Eureka dome tent with a lifetime guarantee. Although I paid double over what I wished to spend, I felt a sense of security knowing that if anything happened to the tent I could get it replaced at any Eureka dealer. After all, this tent was going to be my home for the next year!

As soon as I got home, I headed for the backyard and successfully erected the tent by myself in five minutes. I then waterproofed all the seams with a sealer and left it up overnight to dry. A waterproof duffel bag held my sleeping bag and clothes. My sleeping bag was designed to keep me warm down to zero degrees. My self-inflatable Thermorest air mattress would give me extra comfort after a long day's ride. The duffel bag fit right across the back seat on my bike where it also would serve as a backrest. In addition, I had two saddlebags in which to store more gear: a flashlight, tools, rain suit, road atlas, toiletries, and a first aid kit. Although I was camping, I decided to eat in restaurants mainly because I didn't see how I could fit a camp stove, pans, and food on my bike. After sorting through the rest of my personal belongings, I reduced what I wanted to keep down to six boxes. My daughter, who lived near Orlando, Florida, stored those boxes for me. I sold everything else.

I had no route planned for my trip other than to avoid the northern snowy states in the winter. Because I had no itinerary, I applied for a telephone calling card so I could keep in touch with family and friends without having to call collect. I promised my best friend I would call once a week. I had all my mail forwarded to her post office box and gave her phone number to my family and friends so she could relay messages between us.

The last step entailed planning my budget for the year. I figured I would need about $35 per day. I planned on traveling an average of 150 miles a day, which on *Bessie* would cost me about $5. The cost of camping in state and national parks would generally run around $10 a night. That left me with $20 a day for food and anything else I needed. I decided to purchase $12,000 worth of traveler's checks, which would allow me a budget of $1000 per month. A friend suggested that I join AAA Auto Club in order to buy my travelers checks. Although AAA services would not meet my needs as a motorcyclist, I did save about $300 on the service charge for the traveler's checks. I'll never forget the feeling I had at holding that $12,000 in my hand, seeing the fruit of my hard work and perseverance. I remembered to thank God who had sustained me during the times I had felt like giving up.

The hardest part of preparing for the trip was telling everybody in Daytona Beach good-bye. I called my fifteen-year-old son who lived with his father and stepmother in California, to tell him I was on my way! My daughter was happy for me that I was fulfilling my dream, but she was concerned about when or if I was coming back! A lot of my friends were concerned about me going alone and wondered why I was leaving so close to wintertime. After listening to all their fears and doubts, I felt reassured after discussing my dream trip with my priest. Without a whole lot of explanation, he seemed to understand the nature of my trip. With his blessing, I felt an inner confidence that I had chosen the correct path for my life.

Ten days before I was leaving on *The Joyride*, I stopped by to visit my partying buddies. Every weekend their back yard turned into a non-stop party from Friday night until Sunday. They had an open outdoor bar covered by a thatch roof where everyone gathered. Mostly bikers including a few Vietnam Vets hung out there. Often, the guys would go fishing on Saturdays, which meant that evening there would be a feast, including buckets of clams, for everyone. Typical of our weekend parties, my girlfriend and I shared a few drinks together while the usual crowd stopped in and out. When it began to rain, my friend insisted that I wasn't going to ride my bike home on the wet roads especially since I'd been drinking. We argued about it for a few minutes, but I gave up when I saw two of the guys wheel *Bessie* into the fenced back yard. Since I knew I was there for the night, I partied carefree.

As the night progressed, the thought of having a man to lie with and hold me sounded real comforting. I had been sitting next to Montana, a good-looking man with warm, sensitive eyes, who was always the life of the party. Boldly, I leaned over and asked, "Could you do me a favor? Could you wrap one arm and one leg around me tonight—no sex?"

Montana jumped up and looked searchingly into my eyes, "Let me get this straight. You want me to sleep with you and throw one leg and one arm over you—and no sex? Sounds like intimate stuff to me!"

"Well," I asked, "Is that a 'Yes' or a 'No'?"

His eyes were sparkling with delight when he answered, "I think I can do that for you."

After everyone left and my friends had gone to bed, Montana and I retired to the couch bed. Montana took me in his arms and passionately our lips met in a kiss. My body quickly stirred with feelings and mixed emotions. Although I desired everything he had to offer, I had made a vow to stay celibate until I met my future husband. The last thing I wanted was to have a one-night stand that I would only feel ashamed about in the morning. I gently asked Montana to stop, insisting that he was only frustrating himself. I was shocked when he respectfully stopped and went to sleep. Coming from a childhood background with sexual abuse, I'd had a pattern of picking men who did not respect me. I lay nestled in Montana's arms while my mind raced in a million directions. In only ten days, I was embarking on a journey all by myself. I began to rationalize that one last fling couldn't hurt. Besides, we'd been friends for at least a year. And after all, I could start over with my vow when I left. To Montana's delight, I woke him up and we satisfied our desires that had been ignited earlier. Afterwards, I fell asleep in his arms, content and happy. Several times throughout the night, I woke up to find Montana still awake, holding and stroking me tenderly. It felt so good to be loved. He was holding me like he never wanted to let me go. Then reality hit me. How could he love me? Having a one-night stand isn't love; it's lust. Well, it sure felt like more than lust to me. Confusion took over and I fell asleep wishing that what I felt could be real and not just my imagination.

In the morning our friends fixed us breakfast. Montana wanted to know if he could spend more time with me. I replied, "I have ten days before I leave—they're all yours!" He spent the night at my house that night where we lavished all our attention on each other. We were both starved for the tender touch of a lover. After I gently massaged Montana from head to toe with hot oil, he embraced me in his arms. As he kissed my lips softly, an insatiable desire welled up inside me. We spent the night in wild abandon satisfying each other's passions. The next morning as we were leaving my house, a neighbor man whose advances I had rejected shouted over, "Hey, I thought you didn't like one-night stands?"

I defensively replied, "I don't—this is a ten-night stand!"

I was really enjoying the time I spent with Montana. Every time I thought of him, he brought a smile to my face. We had a whirlwind romance that had both our heads spinning.

One night I asked Montana to drive us down to the beach. We found a secluded spot away from all the motels and condos that grace most of the beach. I spread out the sleeping bag and we both quickly shed our clothes. Laughing, we chased each other down to the water where we frolicked and played, falling down into the waves as carefree as a couple of children. After a moonlit stroll along the beach, we found our sleeping bag and made sweet tender love with the roar of the waves in the background and the twinkling stars shining in the sky. I longed to hear him say the words, "I love you" but they were not yet to come. Each night we were together my feelings for him grew. I began to wonder what it was going to feel like to have to say good-bye.

Two nights before I was to leave Montana proclaimed his love for me noting how different I was from the women in his past. But when I asked him to come with me on *The Joyride* he declined because he didn't have any money to take on the trip. In addition, he was living with his father who was recovering from a second leg amputation. But he did promise to meet me in a couple of months in Las Vegas. That sounded great to me. I would get the best of both worlds: some time to myself and then some time with a man I was falling in love with.

The following night Montana asked me for the keys to *Bessie*. He had sold his motorcycle eight years earlier to divorce himself from the outlaw biker lifestyle.

"What are you going to do?" I asked.

"See if I still remember how to ride!" he replied.

I gave him a quick explanation of *Bessie's* controls and off he rode. A few minutes later he returned motioning for me to climb on. I climbed on the back and we headed off for the backcountry roads that I had ridden so often when I was getting familiar with *Yamabomber.* Every time we came to a stop, the bike was so wobbly I thought for sure that we were going to dump. But we didn't. On the way home, we stopped at a bar for a drink and played a few games of pool. It seemed that no matter where we were or what we were doing, we had so much fun together. I wondered if he could be my "Adam."

Without any forethought, I blurted out, "I have $12,000. Come with me on my trip."

Montana's mouth dropped open. After an awkward period of silence he replied, "I'm really flattered. I've never had anyone offer me anything like this before. I'll have to think about it." With his mom's blessing, the next day he agreed to go.

The purpose of *The Joyride* was more than just an adventurous trek across America by motorcycle—it was a search for answers. It felt like every time I found some peace and stability in my life, some crisis came rolling along like a bowling ball plowing me over as easily as a bowling pin. Why did God allow these things to happen to me? Why did I seem to make the same mistakes over and over again (especially in relationships) expecting different results? Discouraged and frustrated, I was hoping that spending a year traveling alone would help me to discover a personal relationship with God that would sustain me through any crisis! Since Montana had experienced similar frustrations in his life, he agreed that growing in a relationship with God and overcoming our addictions would be good for him as well. But I didn't want to take Montana with me unless he was serious about his intentions. So I asked him if he had thought about marrying me. Montana had that same look of shock he had the first night I had asked him to wrap one arm and one leg around me! He answered with a smile that he had thought about it and promised to marry me by the end of *The Joyride.*

Before Montana and I could leave, we needed to figure out how to add a passenger and more gear on *Bessie.* A friend helped us out by attaching a board on top of our luggage rack, which made enough room for both the tent and duffel bag, thereby freeing up the back seat for a passenger. We then headed over to Montana's home to pick up the clothes he needed. Beside his bed was a Bible with a leather cover that had a soldier engraved on it. In surprise I picked up the Bible. Upon opening it, I found it had been marked up from cover to cover, evidence that it had been well read. I held the Bible up to Montana and inquired, "Is this yours?" He replied that it was and suggested we take it with us. I knew then deep within my heart that *The Joyride* was truly going to be an adventure for both of us.

CHAPTER 3
GOOD-BYE MEANS HELLO

Isaiah 40:31
But those who hope in the Lord will renew their strength.
They will soar on wings like eagles.

Sunday, Halloween Day 1993, *The Joyride* began. We started the day by attending the baptismal service for a good friend's baby. During the service, I recalled with anxiety the promise I had made to myself to give up my habits at the start of my trip. I knelt down to pray, begging God for deliverance from cigarettes, pot, and alcohol. I was surprised when I felt a warm sensation travel throughout my body, filling me with an incredible sense of peace. I knew then that God had answered my prayer.

Following the service, Montana and I headed over to our partying buddy's house to load up our bike. He demonstrated the art of using bungee cords as he strapped down all our gear. Outfitted in all leather, we gave our last hugs and good-byes to our friends who had gathered around. Then we started *Bessie* up with a roar. The last thing I heard as we drove off was a neighbor exclaiming, "Look at that, she's packing on her own bike!" (Packing means riding as a passenger.)

As we headed down the highway, I felt as free as an eagle soaring through the sky. I had everything in life I wanted: a man I loved, *Bessie,* the travelers' checks in my pocket and our camping gear on the back. I didn't know anyone who had set out on a trip of this length before. The only plans I had were to stop and visit some family and friends throughout Florida before we left the state. Knowing it would be a whole year before I would see them again, I wanted one last chance to express my love to them in case anything happened to me during the trip.

We only had to ride twenty-five miles to reach my daughter's house near Orlando. Upon pulling in her driveway, I was touched to find the pumpkin I had given her the week before carved with a zany happy face. Her boyfriend had built a bonfire in the yard. There was a bowl of candy waiting for the expected trick-or-treaters. Since they were going to a Halloween party at Universal Studios, we were left in charge. Montana and I found a bottle of white zinfandel in the refrigerator. Knowing this would be my last night to drink, we poured ourselves a glass before heading out to light the bonfire. As we snuggled close, Montana and I spent the evening watching the flames dance and flicker in the darkness, anticipating the adventure that lie before us.

The next morning I woke up to hear Montana say, "Do you know you are totally gorgeous?" That is the way he woke me up every morning. As Montana and I fixed breakfast for all of us, we visited with the kids. I was thankful that my daughter and I were talking again. Just a year earlier, my daughter had left home at sixteen after deciding that she couldn't abide by my house rules. It broke my heart to see her choose what I knew from experience was a difficult road, but I also knew that she would have to learn for herself just like I had. What made the break even more difficult was that she didn't communicate with me for nine months. She had now been on her own with her boyfriend for a year, however, and I felt confident that she was capable of taking care of herself. I could now relate to the saying that mothers give their children two gifts: roots and wings! After breakfast, I said my hardest good-bye to my daughter.

As we headed towards my parents' home in Venice on Florida's Gulf Coast, the unseasonably cold temperature of fifty-five degrees surprised us. Because of the wind chill factor while riding a motorcycle, it felt much colder. We realized our leather coats and chaps were not enough protection against the cold. I made a mental note to purchase some thermal underwear.

When we arrived at my parents' home, my mother, as usual, had a delicious dinner prepared for us. My Aunt Frances also joined us for dinner. Afterwards, my father entertained Montana with our silent black and white home movies beginning with the day in 1956 that I was brought home from the hospital. When it was time for bed, my parents sent us to separate bedrooms. This was the first night Montana and I had slept apart. Even though at the time I didn't understand why it was wrong for us to sleep together, I respected my father, a retired Presbyterian minister, who was upholding God's moral code, which doesn't change with the generations. When I tried to explain this concept to my daughter, she wrinkled up her nose and declared, "Oh Mom, this is the nineties!"

After my mother had shown us the jewelry that she had made from shark's teeth, we decided to spend the next morning shark tooth hunting at Venice's beaches. It was relaxing walking up and down the beach finding the fossilized shark's teeth in the sand as the gulf waves rolled in and out lapping at our feet. We were free at last—for at least a year—from time pressures, schedules, jobs, and the normal everyday stresses. After saying good-bye to my parents, we headed to Tampa where I wanted to introduce Montana to Anthony and Karol. I had met them a couple years earlier at the Chosen Warriors annual weekender. The event was held on a 400-acre ranch that provided plenty of room for barbecues, hayrack rides, swimming, and field games. Because the Chosen Warriors are a Christian motorcycle club, there was also plenty of opportunity for worship and Bible study. The love and closeness among the club members impressed me so I was delighted when Anthony, the club president, invited me to their next club meeting in Tampa. I would ride over one weekend a month and stay with Anthony and Karol. I was quickly accepted by the group, which provided me with a sense of belonging I needed at that time in my life.

Montana and I spent a couple of days visiting with Anthony and Karol. Karol was amazed that I was content to just sit around and visit. She commented to Montana that he must have a calming effect on me since I was usually the first one to suggest that everyone go out for a ride.

After our visit, we headed over to the other side of Tampa to say our final farewell to my sister Charen and her family. My sister was the first born and I the last born in a family of six children. Following Charen's suggestion, my parents later adopted two more children: a five-year-old Chinese girl from a Hong Kong orphanage and a six-year-old Black girl from foster care. Although there are fourteen years between my sister and I, I feel closer to her than any other member of my family and we keep in touch regularly. Her love, encouragement, and support have helped me through some difficult times. We only visited one night with Charen because she was preoccupied with the birth of her first granddaughter and we were anxious to begin our adventure of *The Joyride.* Feeling satisfied that I had said good-bye to everyone in Florida; I looked forward to visiting the rest of my brothers and sisters who lived throughout the United States. I smiled as I remembered the saying: "Every good-bye is the beginning of a new hello."

CHAPTER 4
WHICH STATE WILL BE BEST?

Psalm 119:105
Your word is a lamp to my feet and a light for my path.

I knew when I was planning my trip around the Unites States by motorcycle that the trip wouldn't be all fun, especially when facing inclement weather. But the one thing I hadn't planned on was getting sick. I had developed a sore throat in Tampa and by the time we rode 200 miles to our first campground near Cedar Key, Florida, I was exhausted. I barely had enough energy left to set up camp before lying down to take a nap. After dreaming about this trip for such a long time, it was difficult to accept that I was sick on our first night of camping especially since I knew we were only heading into colder weather.

To cheer me up after my nap, Montana took me into Cedar Key for a romantic dinner at a restaurant overlooking the ocean. We decided to order one last seafood dinner before bidding farewell to our home state of Florida. When my dinner was served, my first swallow of shrimp was so painful that I couldn't even enjoy my food. Later, Montana took me for a stroll along the docks, but I was feeling so weak I asked him to take me back to the campground.

Not long after we snuggled into our sleeping bag, we were jolted awake by the wildest, spine-tingling screeching that I'd ever heard! We quickly zipped down the back window of our tent just in time to see two raccoons fighting. I huddled next to Montana as we watched the fight feeling grateful I wasn't alone! The fight didn't last too long and the nighttime peacefulness was once again restored. Safe in Montana's arms, I quickly fell back asleep until 4:30 a.m. when we were once again suddenly awakened—this time by a violent windstorm. I imagined we were inside a gigantic lung as I watched our tent walls breathe in and out from the pressure of the wind. Eventually, Montana had to go out into the bad weather to fix one side of the tent blown loose by the battering wind.

We awoke later that morning to calmer winds, thankful that our tent was still standing! However, it was now raining a steady gentle drizzle. As I listened to the raindrops hitting the tent, I couldn't believe how my long awaited dream trip was beginning: suffering from a sore throat; tired after a poor night's sleep due to wild animals and a wind storm, and now rain! We decided to pack up anyway and ride to Florida Caverns State Park about 225 miles north. Pelted by raindrops as we were breaking camp, I wondered if all my years of fantasizing about *The Joyride* had been just that—a fantasy. I secretly hoped the rain would stop. The idea of riding all day through the rain only to set up a wet tent to sleep in sounded like a good recipe for pneumonia!

After riding most of the morning through rain, we stopped for lunch at a roadside café. We ordered two bowls of steaming soup to warm up our chilled bodies. As soon as he finished eating, Montana was ready to head out again. But I insisted we relax in the café a while so I could warm up before heading back into the dreary weather. I didn't dare complain—after all, this entire trip had been my idea!

Fortunately, not long after lunch we rode past the rain clouds into the welcoming sunshine. Upon arriving in the state park, it didn't take us long to set up camp since Montana and I fell naturally into a routine. After we pitched the tent, Montana would escort me to the bathroom so I could inflate our queen size air mattress with my hair dryer. Montana wouldn't let me go anywhere without him insisting it wasn't safe for me to be alone. He even went so far as to come into the restrooms with me to make sure no one was waiting inside to harm me. I resented his overprotection at first. After all, originally I was crossing the whole United States by myself! But when I realized his concern for me was born out of love and not a desire to control me, I began to appreciate him. I even started teasing Montana that God had given me my own personal bodyguard. Once the air mattress was filled, Montana would help me carry it back to the tent. While I made up our bed, Montana would empty the rest of the contents out of the duffle bag onto the tent floor. Since each piece of clothing had been rolled up military style in order to fit everything into the duffle bag, it was necessary to re-arrange our clothes into neat piles around the tent so we could find what we needed. Next, we would both collect firewood for our nightly campfires before we headed to the showers together to wash away the day's road dirt. After cleaning up, we would find a restaurant for dinner unless we had bought something earlier that we could cook over our campfire. Most campgrounds were deserted due to the fall season, giving us the feeling that we had our own private playground in the woods.

Some of my best memories of *The Joyride* are the quiet times Montana and I spent around our campfires talking for countless hours. We learned about each other's past, our hopes and dreams, our fears, as well as our expectations for our future together. Sitting around the campfire night after night without television, telephones, or family and friends to distract us, enabled us to develop a love and intimacy for each other that I had only dreamed about, but never before experienced. It is around our campfires that we began our spiritual journey together studying the Bible and discussing how we could apply God's word into our lives. But our evenings weren't all seriousness. We had lots of fun playing the few games I had brought along on the trip by flashlight. We usually ended the evening by making passionate love before falling asleep content in each other's arms. Montana joked that he looked forward to making love in every state wondering which state would be best!

By the second week of November, we had reached Oak Mountain State Park near Pelham, Alabama. Since the trees still held their beautiful fall colors, we decided to stay a couple of days to explore the state park. Knowing we would be rewarded with a colorful view of the fall foliage, we headed to the summit of Oak Mountain. As we approached the top, the paved road narrowed to a gravel one-lane path. Apparently no one else had chosen to enjoy this autumn day on the mountain as we left all evidence of human civilization behind us in the park below. But when we arrived at the top of the mountain, we found a middle-aged woman sitting alone on a park bench. Seeing the woman by herself reminded me of the times in my life when I had sought solitude by going alone to my favorite places in the woods. After apologizing for interrupting the peace and tranquility, I asked her if she would mind taking our picture. When she snapped the shot for us, we told her about the trip we were taking. She responded by explaining that she had come to the mountaintop to escape the mounting pressure from personal problems. I listened as she described her troubles and offered my encouragement, strength, and hope from similar experiences I had been through. She seemed more cheerful the longer we talked. As we were leaving, she declared that she would never forget us. While driving back down the mountain, I pondered the thought that maybe our chance encounter had been no accident.

That evening, I cooked hamburgers and vegetables in foil over the fire, a meal I had learned to cook on Girl Scout campouts as a child. As we cuddled together under the warmth of our sleeping bag that night, Montana praised me for successfully quitting cigarettes, pot, and alcohol all at once noting that I hadn't even been irritable. Montana didn't appear to be having any withdrawal symptoms either. I described to Montana my unusual experience while praying to God for deliverance from those habits the day we left Daytona Beach. However, it was much easier to quit while being away from the people and places where I had usually partied. But I explained to Montana that it helped me if I didn't think or talk about my addictions.

The next morning greeted us with the coldest temperature yet—twenty-nine degrees. When I stepped outside our tent, a hand of frozen air slapped my face. I pulled the hood from my sweatshirt around my head as I forged my way into the woods for firewood. The birds, seemingly unaffected by the brisk cold, were chirping their morning songs. As I walked deeper into the woods the fall aroma awakened my senses. While shuffling through the fallen leaves, I quickly forgot about the firewood. Surging through my soul was an incredible sense of peace and joy. I wanted to run and shout, “I’m free!” but the cold kept my hands glued in my pockets and my shoulders pulled inward to hold in the warmth from my body. Finally, I stopped to gaze at the beauty around me when my eyes rested upon a deer. I watched silently as this gentle creature grazed in the woods. This is why I had taken *The Joyride.* Already I could feel nature cleansing my soul and replacing my tired spirit with new life. I don’t have any idea how long I stood there, but when thoughts of Montana entered my mind I realized he was probably worrying about me. On my way back to the tent, I gathered as much firewood as I could hold.

Soon I had a crackling fire going which lured Montana out of the tent. Our hungry bellies motivated us to break camp quickly. After securing our gear on *Bessie*, Montana tried to start her, but she was so cold even she wouldn’t crank over. The dreadful thought of being stranded in the middle of nowhere began creeping into my mind. I knew that in cold weather oil thickens, so we needed a way to warm it. Then the idea hit me; we took coals from our campfire and laid them underneath *Bessie*. After fifteen minutes, she started right up!

After breakfast, we were soon heading down Highway 80 west toward Mississippi. Although we wanted to take as many back roads as possible so that we could see the “real” America, we had to be careful to choose good highways for safety reasons. With our heavy load, we didn’t want to worry about being thrown off the road by a pothole! Besides the road conditions, I had heard tales about bikers who had been reported missing while riding country roads through the southern states. As we approached the Mississippi state line I began to worry. How would we be treated in the small towns of southern America? After all, I'm sure we looked intimidating dressed in black leather from head to toe especially to people who weren't used to seeing bikers. But my worries soon vanished when we stopped for lunch at *Bob and Bonnie's*. We were impressed by the friendliness of the locals in the restaurant who made us feel right at home. As I savored my lunch of chicken-n-dumplings, black eye peas, and cornbread, I realized these people were more curious about us than afraid. Our waitress even showed us her "Guest Book" which was a collection of signatures from interesting people she had served. After telling us a few stories about some of the people who had signed her book, we felt honored when she asked us to add our signatures. We knew that we'd be one of her stories to her future guests—the couple who was riding around the United States on their Harley-Davidson!

As we headed down the road after lunch, one of our bungee cords snapped loose releasing our brand new air mattress into the wind. I hollered to Montana to pull over. Since the roadway was empty, I walked casually back to rescue the air mattress. Then from out of nowhere a car appeared driven by a little old lady with round glasses who was peering over the top of her steering wheel. She blasted right over our air mattress mortally damaging the nozzle. In less than two weeks, we had gone through three air mattresses! The first one had a defective seam and leaked. We melted the opening to the second one with our hot hair dryer. Now the third had become road kill! We were just thankful that so far the worst thing that had happened to us was bad luck with air mattresses.

Little did we know that this was only the beginning of our air mattress saga. We eventually went through at least seven more before the trip was over!

As we drove along the Mississippi highways we were disgusted by all the trash littering the shoulders. It gave the state an unkempt appearance and I wondered where their state pride was. When we began to pass shacks along the highway, I realized we were entering a poverty stricken area. We passed an old wrinkled black man in his rocking chair on the front porch of one of the dilapidated shacks. I wondered if this place he called home was all that his life had ever known. Knowing our two lives had been worlds apart yet lived in the same country, I had an overwhelming desire to stop and talk to him. I wanted to know how he felt about his life. Did he have hopes and dreams? Or was he content to just watch the world pass by? Did he realize that in those few seconds our lives had crossed how much his presence had affected me? So close—yet so far apart—we kept driving.

After passing miles of littered highways, we began to question what kind of shape Mississippi's state parks were going to be in. However, when we arrived at Clarco State Park we were pleasantly surprised. The campground surrounded a lake whose surface was as smooth as glass. The fall colors reflected off the water giving a warm glow to the campground. But best of all, the campground was empty so we were able to pick the best campsite on the lake. After pitching our tent, we collected enough firewood for a blazing campfire. While our chicken dinner cooked over the fire, an armadillo meandering through our campsite startled us. We appointed him our official camp mascot. This began a camping tradition of choosing an animal for a mascot in each of our campsites throughout the country.

The next morning we awoke at 4:30 a.m. We cuddled in our tent until a brilliant sunrise appeared over the lake. We laughed when the sound of our lovemaking echoed across the lake, at ease knowing that we were alone in the state park—or so we thought. Montana accompanied me to the woman's bathroom so we could shower together. Even though I had checked the bathroom to make sure no one else was using it, halfway through our shower we heard a toilet flush. Montana said, "Uh oh, I'm busted now!" He hurried to finish his shower and waited for me outside. Sure enough, a lady reported hearing a man in the woman's restroom. A park ranger was sent up immediately to investigate. When I came out of the bathroom, I found Montana talking to him. Although the ranger was younger than both Montana and I, he tried to talk with authority as he scolded us for showering together. He even blushed when he told Montana to use the men's bathroom next time, adding that he would have to evict us from the park if we didn't comply. We were embarrassed as he drove off wondering if anyone had reported hearing our lovemaking earlier!

We could have spent more time exploring the southern states, but I was anxious to get out west where I had never been before, so the next day we headed west through Louisiana. I had been to the French Quarter in New Orleans on a family vacation twenty years earlier. After finding out Montana had never been there, I suggested we spend a few hours in the French Quarter sightseeing. Upon arriving there, I was shocked at how the area had deteriorated. After Montana saw a man walking down the street with a bloody nose, he insisted that he didn't feel safe leaving the bike with its gear parked on the street. Disappointed, I stopped a policeman to inquire about leaving our bike parked. The policeman chuckled before telling us that our bike would be stripped in no time. After hearing his reply, Montana was ready to get back on the highway!

Since Montana gets lost in his own bathtub, I'd been appointed the official pathfinder. I directed him back to Interstate 90, but after a few miles I decided we were going the wrong direction. After Montana turned around, we eventually came to a tollbooth where we received confirmation that we were going the right way. So I don't know what possessed me to disregard the advice and tell Montana to turn around anyway. After driving twenty miles the wrong way, I realized that the tollbooth attendant had been right. For the third time I asked Montana to reverse directions. By this time, he was getting pretty frustrated with me, but he took the next exit anyway with plans to make a u-turn. To our dismay, that exit led to another highway taking us even farther out of the way! Montana immediately took the next exit on that highway and then pulled the bike over to the side of the road. I climbed off the bike laughing nervously at the thought that neither one of us had the faintest idea where we were. Montana just sat on the bike staring at me with a blank look on his face. I was waiting for him to unleash an angry barrage of words, but to my surprise he didn't. I was learning that Montana has incredible patience. When my laughing fit subsided, I climbed back on the bike. After asking for directions, we found our way back to Interstate 90.

I leaned back on *Bessie* relieved that we were finally heading the right way. I was only lost in my daydreams a few minutes when I looked up in shock to see Montana taking an exit.

"What are you doing?" I screamed too late. "You're going the wrong way."

"Uh oh, we're in trouble now!" Montana replied. I looked over to see what he was looking at. There beneath the overpass was an abandoned car, which had been stripped including the tires, with all the windows broken out. I begged Montana to turn *Bessie* around, but he continued on past blocks of housing projects as we delved deeper and deeper into the poverty stricken area. I imagined a horror movie made about a couple of white bikers who got lost in the ghetto and were hunted down and killed by gang members! Montana didn't ease my fears any when he told me that if we ran into any trouble I should spray my pepper gas, while he shot his gun, adding if that didn't work to run for my life. Fortunately, a cab driver noticed we were obviously lost and flagged us down to give us directions back to the highway. A man who was sitting on the curb across the street hollered over to ask us what street we were looking for. Not thinking, I yelled back an answer.

As he motioned us over, he hollered back, "You're going the wrong way. Come over here and I'll tell you the right way."

When the light turned green, Montana kept going—the right way. I can only imagine what that man would have tried to do to us if we had pulled over! We were both relieved when we finally arrived in Fountain Bleau State Park for the night.

CHAPTER 5
TRUST

Psalm 34:8
Taste and see that the Lord is good; blessed is the man who takes refuge in Him.

As we rested in our tent watching the campfire's flames leaping into the darkness, I thought about our day. Losing our way earlier had painfully reminded me of how I had wandered lost through most of my life, all the while not even realizing it. It was not until I got arrested for possession of marijuana while vacationing in the northeast that I stopped to question the direction my life was headed. Handcuffed, I was led into the jail where I was fingerprinted. Scenes from my life raced through my mind. I remembered the difficulty of raising two children while attending four years of college. After I graduated with a B.S. degree in Medical Technology, I had to pass a grueling six-hour exam in order to obtain my license. Soon after, I was able to secure a job in a hospital working the graveyard shift. The desire to give my children a better life than they could receive growing up on welfare payrolls kept me motivated. As the officer pressed my index finger into the black inkpad, I wondered: was my use of pot going to cost me everything—even my children?

But I got a break. Since I didn't have a previous arrest record, the night court judge turned me loose. My boyfriend, who I was with at the time, wasn't as lucky. He was detained in jail with four felony charges relating to the possession of a concealed firearm. Frightened and alone, I drove back home to Florida in eighteen hours.

The following weeks after my vacation, I sank into a deep depression. It became apparent to me that I had been on a self-destructive path following my divorce. I didn't understand why since I thought my ex-husband had been the cause of all my misery! After struggling with suicidal thoughts, I realized I needed help. My employee health nurse referred me to Dr. Graham, the psychologist available to employees of the hospital where I worked.

During my first appointment, Dr. Graham began questioning me about my childhood. Frustrated and scared, I wanted to escape the cause of my present misery—not think about my past. With reluctance, I shared that I had been sexually abused starting around age six. Dr. Graham suggested beginning my therapy with that experience. Of the three books he recommended, *Courage to Heal: A Guide for Women Survivors of Child Sexual Abuse* affected me the most. I saw myself in the book as I read about other abused women who described growing up with feelings of shame, low self-esteem and fears. I came to understand that I had a six-year-old child living within me who needed healing.

Six months passed before I worked up the courage to go back to Dr. Graham and face my past. He explained that the hurts from my past hung about my neck like a bag full of bricks. Through the process of counseling, I would empty the bag one brick at a time. Eventually, when free of the years of extra weight, my present problems would seem simpler to handle. I took my first step towards recovery by giving up pot and alcohol, a step Dr. Graham insisted necessary to assure my emotional healing.

Over the next year I continued to see Dr. Graham while also attending a twelve-step program he had recommended. I felt troubled during the early twelve-step meetings when I heard other members talking about turning their lives over to God. After all, where was God when I was getting molested?

Not long after I started recovery, all the pain, bitterness and anger that had been bottled up inside me all those years, erupted into a flood of tears—tears that lasted three long days. If this was all life had to offer I didn't want to live. Nobody had explained to me that when delving into past hurts it was a normal reaction to have a flood of emotions. Having been to my twelve-step group a few months, I knew this was the time I should reach out and call somebody on the phone list that had been provided to me. But who would want to listen to me? All I had to offer was pain and I couldn't see an end to it. As my thoughts dragged me lower and lower, I finally got out of bed and grabbed my gun from the closet. While holding it I contemplated putting a bullet through my head. Visions of my slumped body lying in a pool of blood flashed through my mind. Who would be the one to find my dead body? Realizing that it would probably be one of my children, I cried out, "Oh God, if you really are out there and if you really want me to live, then you better send someone over here to stop me because I just don't want to hurt anymore and I'm too scared to reach out to someone." What was I expecting—a miracle? Nobody ever stopped by to see me. I had kept myself isolated. No sooner had that thought crossed my mind than I heard a knock at my door. In unbelief, I walked to my front door and opened it. There stood an ex-boyfriend uttering an explanation that he had no idea why he was there. I did! I knew then without a doubt that there was a God...He was listening to me...and He wanted me to live.

I called my sister Charen the next day to share what was happening in my life. She helped me to resolve my bitterness toward God by pointing out that He is not responsible for the evil actions of people because He created all of us with free will to make our own choices. She further explained that when people choose not to follow God they become selfish gratifying their desires no matter who it hurts. When I quit blaming God for the way my life had turned out, I was ready to accept His love. But I felt as if I had to do something to earn it. What was there to love about me? It seemed all I had done was make a mess out of my life with poor choices. That's when Charen began teaching me about God's grace. The Bible says, *"For it is by grace you have been saved, through faith—and this not from yourselves, it is the gift of God—not by works, so that no one can boast" (Eph. 2:8-10).*

In spite of my growing belief that I was loved and accepted by God, I was still afraid of getting close to people. Once again Charen encouraged me by explaining, "Joy, as a child you were hurt through the hands of a man, but you will also be healed through the hands of a man, God can't do it all, you need to reach out to people—you need God with skin on!" Slowly, with the help of my twelve-step group, I came to believe that there were trustworthy people.

During this healing process, God brought some very special friends into my life. I met Linda at one of my twelve-step groups. I could tell by comments she had made that she was a Christian. After a meeting one night, I bravely approached her and asked her what church she attended. I wanted to find "God with skin on" as my sister had suggested, but I was afraid. Would I find the love and acceptance in her church that I had discovered through my private relationship with God, or would the church members try to dictate how God wanted me to talk, dress and act which had happened to me once before. Linda invited me to attend with her that Sunday, but fear of people's judgment and religious control kept me from going. A few weeks later, Linda invited me again, but this time to a Christian twelve-step group she had started at her church. The idea of being able to name my God as Jesus Christ instead of the generic Higher Power required at twelve-step meetings excited me. This time I accepted her invitation. I liked the meetings so much that I continued with them, but I ended up following a boyfriend into the Catholic Church. The twelve-step program and the Catholic Church guided my life over the next three years. Not only did I begin to enjoy life, but also for the first time in a long time, I started to feel good about myself. A pop from the fire startled me out of the past. I got up to zip the tent closed before curling up next to Montana for a peaceful night's sleep.

As we headed down the highway the next day, Montana and I looked for the Crawfish Kitchen, which had been recommended by some neighboring campers. The sky had been threatening rain all morning. The wind gusts made it difficult for Montana to keep *Bessie* on a straight path. Only the thought of food kept us going! Finally, we spotted the restaurant. Their seafood bar had all the Louisiana Cajun food you could imagine—and of course all the crawfish you could eat. Our waitress laughed at the fact that she had to show us how to find our way to the meat of the crawfish.

While back at the food bar for seconds, Montana struck up a conversation with an older woman. When he told her I was writing a book about our trip, she left Montana at the food bar, came to where I was sitting, and introduced herself. Frances handed me a printed card with a poem she had written and said I could put it in my book:

TRUST

T*ragedy occurred.*
He came.
R*estless sleep.*
He comes.
U*nresolved conflicts.*
He comforts, strengthens.
S*tandard guidance needed.*
His way is secure, safe, and best.
T*rust Him.*
His name is Jesus.

He is my way, my truth, and my life.
I can do all things through Him.

Frances explained that she had been in a horrible car wreck, which had killed her husband. While she lay grieving in the hospital over the next nine months, the word *trust* kept popping into her head, followed by the words of her poem. Perhaps she merely wished to share her own story and get it published. Maybe she was wise enough to know that everyone meets tragedy in their lives and needs to learn to trust in God. Or perhaps the memory of my own tragedies still showed in my eyes. I didn't really understand why she gave me the poem or told me her story, but I thanked her as I put the poem in my back pocket.

After we finished stuffing ourselves, Montana and I headed to Lake Fausse Point State Park where we set up camp just in time to escape the downpour, which had shadowed us all day. When a motorcycle pulled into the campground later that night, I felt unusually curious. I wanted to meet our soul mates that were as crazy as we were to be traveling by motorcycle and camping in the rain!

We headed in the dark over to their campsite. To our surprise, the couple was from Germany, also traveling around the United States for a year on their motorcycle. Although I was excited to meet them, I felt a little jealous this couple from a foreign country was touring my own country that even I hadn't seen yet, and they were so young! I pouted—behind my usual polite manner—with a tinge of self-pity, I think, as I counted the years it had taken me to save for this trip. Although they struggled with the English language, we all talked a while. Then we said good-bye and wished them a safe trip.

The next morning it was still raining quite hard. The weather report forecasted rain for the next five days with flash flood warnings. I didn't really want to ride in the rain, but we figured the only way to get past the rain was to ride through it. (I reflected with a crooked smile about how true that had been in facing my emotional pain—the only way to get out of it was to work through it!) Reluctantly, we packed up and rode one hundred miles through a hard rain. We passed flooded fields slowly encroaching upon the roadside. Every bump we hit seemed harder than the last and I worried we had broken a shock. From my listing of Harley-Davidson dealerships, I found one in Lake Charles, Louisiana where we could have the back shock checked and get *Bessie* a tune-up. It was a good time to find a motel room for the night and dry out.

We walked into the Harley dealership dripping wet. Fortunately, they were able to service our bike right away. In the waiting area we stripped out of our rain gear and leather down to a dry layer of clothes. While we were waiting, another couple came in the shop. Because the woman did not stop laughing from the time she walked through the door, I whispered to Montana that she sounded stoned. Eventually they worked their way around to where we were sitting and struck up a conversation with us. When they learned we were waiting for our bike they invited us out for a drink. To my surprise Montana accepted the offer. Before I had a chance to object, we were following them out to their pickup. Since I had only abstained from alcohol for three weeks, I knew I wasn't strong enough to sit in a bar without ordering a drink. Upon arriving at the bar, Linda bought us each a drink. By the end of the hour, I was not only on my second drink but smoking Linda's cigarettes, too.

When we thought *Bessie* would be ready, we returned to the Harley shop. Our bumpy ride had been caused by only seven pounds of pressure in our back tire, which holds thirty pounds when full. On our way out, Linda and Fred asked us out again, insisting that we could spend the night in Fred's travel trailer that he kept parked behind his house. Knowing that we would save money by not getting a motel room, we agreed. Since Linda wanted a ride on the bike, Montana suggested I ride her over to the bar while he rode with her boyfriend in the pickup. Although I could not easily respond, I listened to Linda talk non-stop into one ear about the pain and loneliness in her life.

Upon arriving at the bar, we played a few games of pool while the guys visited at a nearby table. Linda bought us drinks faster than we could finish them and it wasn't long before both of us were drunk. Heads turned when we started dancing freely around the bar. Before the night was over, Linda dragged me into the bathroom where she cried hysterically. As I listened to her complain about her life, I thought about Frances' poem. I pressed the poem into Linda's hand and suggested she read it in the morning. Linda took the poem and said she wanted to leave. Since Montana appeared the only sober one in our group, I asked him if he would drive her home, but Montana did not want to leave me alone in the bar. Linda's boyfriend insisted he'd watch out for me so to hold him to his word Montana asked the man for his wallet until he returned. I couldn't believe it when the man handed it over. With the wallet in hand, Montana headed out the door with Linda. I hadn't even finished playing a game of pool with Linda's boyfriend, when Montana stormed back into the bar ranting and raving that Linda wouldn't keep her hands to herself. I didn't get upset for two reasons: one, the episode increased my respect and trust in Montana, and two; I understood that Linda was literally grasping for anything to take away her emotional pain. Linda approached me with the $60 sweater she had purchased earlier in the Harley shop, offering it to me as an apology. But I didn't need her sweater or her apology. Linda and her boyfriend began arguing until she stomped out of the bar in the arms of another man. I've often wondered what ever happened to her.

I only hope that the poem I passed on encouraged her to trust in the Lord Jesus Christ.

We stayed that night in Fred's travel trailer. I was shocked when he invited me into his home to meet his wife! I didn't think the night could get any crazier until we walked in to find his wife crying hysterically. He asked us to leave them alone. Later, he came out to the travel trailer to explain that his wife of twenty years was crying because he had told her earlier that he was divorcing her.

Before heading out the next morning, we left our host a thank you note. As we rode towards my sister's home in Houston, Montana and I agreed not to ever separate again while on *The Joyride.* Not only did we not want to worry about other people getting between us, but we realized that if something happened to one of us, the other would have no way of knowing. Now that we had fallen deeply in love, it was frightening to think about losing each other in the middle of the U.S.A.

CHAPTER 6
DON'T MESS WITH TEXAS

1 Corinthians 15:33
Do not be misled: Bad company
corrupts good character.

On the ride to Darlene's, my adopted black sister, I reminisced about the mid-sixties when she first came to live with my family. We lived in an all-white neighborhood, attended all-white schools, and an all-white church. But I was thrilled with her adoption—now I could pass on the *baby of the family* title. I proudly accepted my big sister responsibility of escorting Darlene back and forth to school.

As we walked home from our first day of school, a boy ran across the street screaming at my sister, "You dirty bald-headed nigger!"

Tears welled up in her eyes as Darlene said to me, "But I'm not bald."

"That just shows you how stupid he is," I replied.

At ten years of age, I was introduced to prejudice, an attitude that went against everything I had ever known. My parents had always modeled a love for people, especially children, regardless of their appearance or background. Even though my parents had six children of their own, they opened their home to five more children over the years. In 1959, when I was three years old, my parents adopted a Chinese orphan from a Hong Kong orphanage. In 1961, during my fifth year, my parents invited an African exchange student to spend a summer with us. The next year they hosted three Cuban refugee children brought to the United States through a government program called Operation Peter Pan. Unfortunately, their parents were detained in Cuba, so what was supposed to be a six-week commitment extended to two years. Finally, in 1966 at ten years of age, my black sister Darlene came to live with us. Although I had been exposed to different races and cultures of people since I was three years old, I'd never been exposed to prejudice before.

Thankfully, Darlene and I didn't experience any more negative incidents on our walks home from school after a group of Catholic students next door to my public school found out what had happened. They watched out for us on our walks home and it felt good to have some "protection." Oddly, the little boy and my sister became neighborhood friends. It was only later in life that my father explained to me why our family had been unable to spend that summer swimming at our local country club where we had been members for years. When the owner of the club learned of my black sister's adoption, he kicked my family out of the club. My father successfully fought the owner's decision by getting a petition signed by other club members threatening to quit the club if we weren't let back in!

When we arrived at Darlene's home in Houston, her son, Jimmy, greeted us. Soaking wet from riding through a torrential downpour, we changed into some dry clothes. As we waited for Darlene to arrive home from work, we watched the television news reporting that a tornado had touched down in Houston damaging an apartment building. I felt grateful we had arrived safely! Montana jokingly referred to *Bessie* as our surfboard as he recalled riding the gigantic walls of water thrown up by the tractor-trailers on the highway.

We stayed with Darlene's family for four days. We reminisced about our childhood and shared the new events in our lives. Except for the one night we all went out to dinner, Montana and I spent most of our time resting up from all our travels. I enjoyed cooking and cleaning for Darlene while she was at work, which made me realize that I was missing having a home of my own.

The morning we left Houston, I noticed that our back tire looked low again. After filling it up with air, we headed for the next Harley dealership in order to get the tire checked out. This time the mechanic found a nail in our back tire. It was scary knowing we had ridden several days with a damaged tire. A couple who worked at the shop offered to let us stay in their trailer on the gulf coast beach that night, but the offer had a familiar ring which made us graciously, but instantly decline! As they saw us off, they recommended the free camping on the beach and a great place to get steaks in Quintana, Texas.

When we arrived on the Texas gulf coast, we explored the possibility of camping on the beach, but found it dirty, polluted, and too close to the water—high tide would have easily washed us away. Instead we camped in a county park located in the middle of Quintana. Quintana, with its claim to fame being it was the first place white man set foot in Texas, has a mere population of only fifty-one. Even so, I thought it strange there was not even one church in town.

It wasn't hard to locate the Sandbar and Grill which treated us to the biggest, tastiest T-bone steaks we had ever eaten, and I imagine will ever eat again. While we were savoring every bite, we questioned our waitress about the area. She replied that she knew someone who could answer our questions better than her. A few minutes later, a woman in her mid-forties appeared at our table introducing herself as the mayor of Quintana. She invited us to come join her when we finished with our meal.

Eager to get to know the local people, we pulled up our chairs at the mayor's table where we met her husband. They bought us a couple of drinks while they entertained us with stories about their lives in Quintana. It wasn't long before the restaurant/bar began filling up with people. It is quite likely we met the whole town of Quintana!

As the night progressed, the restaurant became nosier and livelier in proportion to the amount of alcohol being consumed. I had fun just observing the people participating in this small town Friday night ritual. It didn't take me long though to realize that it wasn't much different than any other Friday night in a Daytona Beach bar. I had taken *The Joyride* to get away from this lifestyle so I was beginning to ask myself what I was doing there. Then the mayor caught my attention when she asked the group at our table if we wanted to see her new tattoo. As she stood up and began unbuttoning her pants, she explained the tattoo was a mouse. I began to get uncomfortable wondering what she was going to do next when she peeked down her pants exclaiming, "Shucks, my pussy ate it!" As everyone roared with laughter at our table, I decided I'd learned enough about Quintana. As we said good-bye to our hosts, the mayor invited us to come back the next night for a toga party.

"What's a toga party?" I asked.

"It's a party you attend wearing nothing more than a sheet!" she answered with a grin.

The next morning we decided to follow the gulf coast to Padre Island National Seashore. Helping Montana fold up the tarp for some reason made me think about square dancing. I still find the thought strange since I had only square danced once in my life as a child at a birthday party. As my corner of the tarp touched Montana's I thought "And dosado!" (A call in square dancing) I was flabbergasted when Montana smiled back and replied, "And dosado to you too!" How did he know what I was thinking?

As we headed down the highway I was thankful for the long hours traveling allowing me to wander and sort through my thoughts as the motorcycle pipes drowned out all other sounds. This particular day I reminisced about all the bitterness and resentments I had harbored for years toward people who had hurt me. I had mistakenly thought that by holding onto the anger I was somehow punishing the people who had gone on to live their lives without me. Only through my twelve-step support group, did I realize the only person being punished by all those negative emotions was myself. That's when I finally understood the Bible teachings on the importance of forgiveness. Forgiveness isn't a favor granted to the offender letting him off the hook; it's a favor to you. The Lord's Prayer says God will forgive us as we forgive others. Forgiving people in my past freed me to experience the joys in my day-to-day life.

During that time of healing, I attended a motorcycle rally where I met Justin. As our friendship developed we realized we had a great deal in common. Although he had lost a leg in the Vietnam War, he relearned to ride a motorcycle. In addition, we both attended twelve-step programs. He was, as well, the first man I had dated since my divorce that both my children liked, and he was looking for a wife! Our friendship turned into romance. Two years later we were married in his Catholic church. I proudly walked down the aisle on the arm of my father hoping this marriage would be different from my first! Following the ceremony and reception, we departed for our honeymoon—a weeklong motorcycle trip through the Florida Keys and Everglades National Park.

Six weeks after our honeymoon, I came home from work to find a manila envelope on the kitchen counter addressed to me. My husband sat in a chair and watched quietly as I opened it up and discovered divorce papers. Needless to say, I packed up and moved all my belongings out the next morning with one exception—my car. I had sold it because Justin owned both a Corvette and a Cadillac and had insisted we didn't need three cars. It's a good thing I loved riding *Bessie* because now she was all I had for transportation. If *The Joyride* was ever going to be a reality I couldn't afford to buy another car. With unshakable determination, I endured adverse weather during the next two years as I rode *Bessie* back and forth to work.

The day after I moved out of Justin's house, I called my best friend. She told me Justin had informed her about the divorce, justifying his actions with the explanation that I was plotting to kill him! When I heard that, I couldn't argue with the fact that Justin was mentally unstable. Why hadn't I seen he was troubled? As I reviewed all the pre-marital preparation the Catholic Church had put us through including counseling, I remembered the compatibility test we had been given. Our priest expressed concern because we had received one of the lowest scores recorded. Although there had been many signs, I later learned that Justin had a mental disability resulting from his service in the Vietnam War, which he had not told me about. This mental disability apparently only manifested during times of stress such as a significant life event like marriage. Justin wasn't responsible for this divorce—we should have never gotten married. I had missed and/or chosen to ignore all the red flags. Denial is a powerful force!

My life felt like the saying: "Life is sometimes like an ice cream cone—as soon as you think you got it licked, it drips all over you!" I began attending my twelve-step meetings daily to help me through my crisis. Even though my daughter encouraged me to date again, I thought it best to stay away from men for a while. To help combat my loneliness and grief I participated every weekend feeding the homeless through the food ministry in the Catholic Church where I had been married. In addition, I became actively involved with the Chosen Warriors, a Christian motorcycle club. I even had the opportunity to serve on a ten-day medical mission to the Dominican Republic thinking that longer medical missions might be something I'd like to pursue in the future. But no matter how involved I became with other Christians, I still felt an aching emptiness when I climbed into bed every night… alone. After battling the loneliness for nine months and feeling like it wasn't getting any easier, my sixteen-year-old daughter moved out and ran off with her boyfriend. My spirit was crushed. It felt like every person I loved had rejected and abandoned me.

About this time I ran into my old boyfriend who I had gotten arrested with three years earlier. He began coming by to see me. Only a couple of months later, out of desperation, I moved back in with him. It wasn't long before I began drinking and smoking pot again. Over the next few months, I slowly dropped out of my church activities and began withdrawing.

My life seemed to parallel the board game *Chutes and Ladders* that I used to play with my children. After almost reaching the top of the board game to become a winner, one roll of the dice can land your playing piece in a chute sending it down to a lower level on the board. As my self-esteem plummeted, I realized that my choice to move in with my ex-boyfriend had been a big mistake, but I didn't have the emotional strength to move out and face living alone. So I did the only thing I knew how to do—cry out to God for help. He answered my prayer when my boyfriend, who just a week earlier had promised to love me forever, suddenly and unexpectedly, moved out. Over the next three months I tried unsuccessfully to give up my use of pot and alcohol. That's when I decided it was time to take *The Joyride.*

I fast-forwarded to the present when Montana pointed out a pig's head that had been stuffed onto a fence post. I wondered why anyone would do something like that! We were really disappointed as we rode along the Texas gulf coast and saw all the oil refineries spouting their obnoxious fumes into the air. What a contradiction to see the State's "Don't Mess with Texas" road signs warning against littering! We were both beginning to realize how much we had taken for granted the beauty of our beaches back home in Florida.

Finally, we came to the ferry that would take us across to Padre Island National Seashore. We decided to spend a few nights there when we found out the camping was free. After setting up camp, we took a walk along the beach and met another couple from Germany, Gitta and Rainer. They were also traveling around the United States for a year but in a van. That night as we were relaxing by our campfire, Gitta and Rainer approached us with a six-pack of beer and asked if they could join us. Rainer held us spellbound as he told us stories about growing up in Communist East Germany and his eventual escape through the guarded wall that separated East and West Germany leaving behind his family and friends. Hearing history from a person who has lived it is much more fascinating than reading about it in grammar school textbooks. I realized that I had taken for granted the freedom I enjoyed as an American Citizen and how important it is to protect our freedoms.

The following morning Montana woke me up to watch a brilliant sunrise over the ocean as he sang me "Happy Birthday." My thirty-seventh birthday is one I'll never forget. We started off the day by exploring one of the nature trails in the park. After hiking through the sand dunes a little while, I looked down just in time to scream at Montana to stop. Being a Vietnam Veteran, he reacted by freezing dead in his tracks with his body weight on the ball of his right foot while his heel was still raised in the air. I probably gave him flash backs of Vietnam; however, it wasn't a land mine underneath his heel but a baby rattlesnake. After I told him about the snake, he slowly stepped away. If he hadn't stopped when I hollered, he would have stepped on it. When we poked at the rattlesnake with a stick, it slithered away into the bush. As we proceeded down the trail, Montana thanked me for saving his life. All of a sudden he leaped three feet into the air; coming at us was a bigger rattlesnake. The snake seemed just as startled to see us and quickly disappeared. Montana claimed that we had just seen baby rattler's big brother and suggested we get off the trail before we ran into daddy rattler! I wondered if I could buy a snakebite kit to add to our first aid supplies.

Having had enough of nature for the day, we decided to head into town for a birthday meal. We found an Italian restaurant, which had one of my favorite appetizers—Escargot. While we were eating, one of the chefs came to our table to see if we were enjoying our food. When he found out that we were traveling around the United States for a year on *Bessie,* he invited us over to his home since he was about to get off work. As soon as we arrived, he fixed us each a drink and offered us his pot pipe. I don't know why I just didn't say no because I didn't even enjoy the high pot gave me anymore. As soon as I smoked the pot, I regretted it. My neck stiffened up with tension as the waves of paranoia hit me...one of the long-term effects of smoking marijuana.

When we were ready to return to our campsite, I was so stoned I couldn't remember how to get there. It was going to be up to Montana to find our way back. He reassured me he could do it. When we had almost reached our destination, for some reason Montana decided to stop alongside the road. After I climbed off the bike, Montana went to get off but forgot to put the kickstand down. Both *Bessie* and Montana went tumbling into the street. Montana was so drunk he didn't even bother to get up but just stayed in the middle of the road laughing. I was so disgusted with the whole situation and wondered how on earth he had driven that far without getting us both killed. I got Montana and the bike off the road and somehow we made it safely back to the tent.

We had planned on continuing *The Joyride* the next morning, but we were both too hung over. That's when I decided I was really finished with partying. Montana didn't believe me until he saw me throw away the pot we had been given the night before. Although God had delivered me from desiring pot or alcohol, I still had a problem just saying no when around people who were using. I knew that in the future I was going to have to be very selective who I socialized with in order to maintain my sobriety. Furthermore, I was discovering the natural high from living my dream and I wanted to be fully sober to enjoy it!

We awoke the following morning, Thanksgiving Day, to a forty degree drop in temperature and gray skies. As we packed up the tent and our belongings, gusts of wind blew sand into everything. It was miserable. We regretted not leaving the day before when it had been a calm, sunny eighty degrees. To make matters worse, it began to drizzle. After riding a hundred miles, we became so chilled we were forced to stop and rent a motel room. As we were checking in, I noticed the Thanksgiving buffet in the motel restaurant. At least we would get a turkey dinner! We went up to our room where we enjoyed the first hot shower in four days. Afterwards, Montana took a nap while I lay next to him watching television. I was startled when I heard someone fiddling with our motel room door. All I could do was gasp in surprise when a man walked right into our locked room. Montana woke up out of a dead sleep when he heard me gasp, grabbed his pistol by the bed and shouted at the man to stop. Montana had reacted so quickly that the intruder slowly backed right out of our room apologizing with each step. I was thankful then for Montana's Vietnam War training, which had saved our lives. He became my hero that day and I felt safe and protected with him.

CHAPTER 7
COYOTES, ROAD RUNNERS, JAVELINAS, OH MY!

Psalm 46:10
Be still and know that I am God.

As we made our way through Texas, I felt small in the midst of the wide-open spaces. All we saw for miles and miles was dry, brown, dusty fields with only cacti and shrubs for vegetation. The small towns were getting smaller and farther and farther apart. I wondered how anyone could enjoy living in this desolate land. However, after talking to some of the locals, we learned that the area was famous worldwide for rattlesnake hunting. When we spotted three coyotes running through the field that morning, I felt we had reached an untamed section of the United States.

Lunchtime, we stopped at a Mexican restaurant in one of the quaint towns. When we walked in, I saw a patron who had a big bowl of soup that looked so good we asked the waitress to bring us each one. When the soup was served, I ate a few bites but began to wonder what kind of meat I was eating because it had an unfamiliar texture. After looking over to see if Montana was eating his soup, I picked a piece of meat out with my spoon. It even looked strange—like a sponge. I asked Montana if he'd ever eaten meat like this before. When he joked back that it was probably road kill, I began to lose my appetite. Finally, I asked the waitress what kind of meat was in our soup. She replied with a heavy Spanish accent, "It's a cow." Since the meat didn't look like any beef I'd ever eaten, I couldn't eat it, but I finished the broth. We were shocked when we received our check for $9 for two bowls of soup.

After lunch, we finally made it to Seminole Canyon State Park where we encountered our first difficulty at erecting our tent. The ground was so hard we couldn't put the stakes in, so Montana came up with the brilliant idea of using bungee cords and rocks to hold our tent down. I wondered if I had been alone if I would have thought of that idea. There was something very different about this area, but I couldn't put my finger on it. After a while, I realized what it was—the absolute silence. I couldn't hear the wind blowing because there weren't any trees. There wasn't any noise from traffic. There weren't even any birds or insects chirping. I sat very still for a few minutes just absorbing the vastness of the land around me in total silence. It was so quiet; my own thoughts rattling around my head seemed to disturb the peace. I wondered what life had been like for the Indians who had lived there years before leaving behind their mysterious pictographs on the canyon walls.

After setting up camp, we headed into Comstock, Texas for dinner. We decided to stick to traditional American food and ordered hamburgers and french fries. We told our waitress about our lunch that day and she replied, "Oh, you had Menudo. They claim it's great for a hangover." When we asked her what kind of meat was in the soup, she explained that it was tripe, a fancy word for cow intestines. Once again, we couldn't believe the price of our meal at $16.

After spending $25 of our $35/day budget on two meals, we decided it was time to do more of our own cooking. We were spending way over our daily budget, and I wanted to make sure we had enough money to last into spring so we could explore the northwestern states that I'd read so much about. So the next morning, Montana surprised me by starting a fire and cooking bacon and eggs in foil over the fire. When he was just about done frying the first batch of bacon, some grease dripped through a hole in the foil sparking a grease fire that burned up his first batch. Undaunted, Montana patiently tried again. I was delighted when he served me my bacon and scrambled eggs, but I suggested maybe it was time to buy a camp stove and pans.

We found a town with a hardware store on the way to our next destination, Big Bend National Park. We bought their last camp stove. I'm sure we were quite a sight as the town folks watched us dump out our duffle bag on the sidewalk. We had to decide which things to mail home in order to make room for the new supplies. We managed to fit more supplies on *Bessie* than I could have ever imagined. We probably looked like the Beverly Hillbillies as we headed down the road with our coffee mugs dangling from the back of our pack.

On the way to Big Bend National Park, Montana was intrigued when we happened upon Langtry, Texas, the home of his hero, the famous Judge Roy Bean. Although he was known as "the law west of the Pecos," we learned on our tour of the original courthouse saloon that the saloonkeeper Judge would often recess trials just to sell liquor to the courtroom. Of course, Montana had to pose for a picture at the bar holding his prized pistol that he had brought back from Vietnam and now carried with us on *The Joyride.*

When we finally arrived at Big Bend, we learned that there were three campgrounds to choose from. We camped in the Rio Grande Village campground because it was along the Rio Grande River with a grocery store and gas station nearby. While we were setting up camp, Montana left me alone while he went to find the bathroom. All of a sudden, a coyote came running right through our campsite. He stopped dead in his tracks when he saw me. I wasn't sure what to do. After we stared at each other for what seemed like eternity, I hollered and waved my hands until the coyote took off running. When Montana came back, I excitedly told him about my experience. Then Montana spotted a roadrunner behind our tent—and I thought roadrunners only existed in cartoons!

Our first night in Big Bend, we were serenaded to sleep by a pack of howling coyotes. The noise scared me at first until I realized the coyotes weren't going to bother us. Just to be on the safe side though, I had Montana cut a Gatorade bottle in half to use as a bedpan so I didn't have to leave the tent in the middle of the night.

The next morning I rode down to the village store to make some phone calls home. I patiently waited for the older gentleman to get done with the phone. When he finished, he asked me for a ride on my motorcycle up to the nearest service station twenty miles away to purchase a fan belt, which had broken in his truck. I went back to the campground and asked Montana if he would help Mac out. Although Mac was in his seventies, he enjoyed his ride on the back of *Bessie*. To show his appreciation, Mac's wife Rachel invited us over for dinner, and each day after that they stopped by our campsite to check on us, bringing us much-appreciated gifts from ice cubes to books. When Montana hurt his back trying to move our picnic table, Rachel even brought over some codeine tablets to help ease the pain that kept Montana immobilized for a couple of days. We enjoyed our visits with Mac and Rachel as they had traveled around the United States for many years in their R.V. and had lots of adventures to share. I was discovering there were quite a few people who spend months traveling the countryside.

One disadvantage to camping in national parks is the lack of showers or hot water, although lately some of the more popular national parks have installed pay showers. It's not easy bathing with cold sink water when the temperatures are only in the twenties and thirties. So we were excited when we discovered the hot springs in the park. We drove down early every morning so we could enjoy the 105-degree crystal clear spring water by ourselves. Thousands of gallons gushed from the hot springs spilling over into the frigid Rio Grande River, which ran alongside it. As I soaked in the soothing hot springs, I thought about J. O. Langford who had homesteaded the land and springs in 1909. He had come to the area when he heard about the spring's acclaimed healing powers hoping to regain his health, which suffered after his many bouts with malaria. Following the treatment used by the Indians, a bath each day for twenty-one days along with drinking some of the spring water, Langford recovered completely. By 1920, he had built a two-story bathhouse over the springs, and began to sell baths in the healing waters to tourists. A few years after a flood in 1938 washed away a portion of the bathhouse, the Langford's sold their property to the state of Texas for eventual donation to Big Bend National Park. All that is left of the bathhouse now is a foundation wall around the springs.

I read the story of Langford's adventurous life in his book, *Big Bend: A Homesteaders story,* while camped at the park. When Montana and I discovered the other hot springs that Langford mentioned in his book, we began to visit it instead.

Since the spring was secluded from view by river reeds, it was a great place for romantic interludes. We knew that we weren't the first tourists to find it as evidenced by the burned candles that had been left behind.

We spent most of our days in Big Bend hiking trails throughout the park. On almost every hike we spotted javelinas, which are wild pigs that look so ugly they're almost cute. As I walked the same trails used years before by the Comanche Indians, I tried to imagine what life had been like for the Indian warriors. Sometimes we met Mexicans who had illegally crossed the Rio Grande River, which separates Mexico from Texas, to sell their handmade wares to tourists. Almost every night we attended a program hosted by a park ranger who taught about the plant and animal life in the desert. The information we learned helped to make our day hikes more interesting.

One of the highlights during our two-week stay in Big Bend was the twenty-mile rafting trip we took down the Rio Grande River through Santa Elena Canyon. Since neither one of us was experienced at rafting, we hired Far Flung Adventures to guide us down the river. When we arrived at their outpost in Terlingua, Texas, we were loaded up into a van pulling a trailer holding our rubber raft. As we bounced along the road to the river, my anticipation of our latest adventure grew. After asking our guide a myriad of questions, he assured us that he had guided hundreds of people down the river. Before we arrived at our loading spot on the river, our driver stopped at a market so we could buy snacks for our trip. When Montana met me at the cash register with a six-pack of beer, I felt a sense of dread. Although I had firmly resolved to stick to my decision not to party, Montana apparently didn't demonstrate the same commitment. But when I heard Montana offer to share the beer with our guide, I figured a few beers couldn't do any harm.

Finally, we arrived at the river where the crew placed our raft into the water. Once all the supplies were loaded we were instructed to climb in. We settled into our seats as our guide pushed us off. While he rowed, he entertained us with stories about the area. By the time we stopped along the riverbank for lunch, Montana had already sucked down four beers. As he stumbled out of the raft, I couldn't figure out why he was so intoxicated. Then it dawned on me that he had taken a couple of codeine tablets that morning which was not a good mixture with alcohol. Even though our guide had prepared a gourmet lunch on top of a folding picnic table including smoked oysters on crackers with cream cheese and Picapeppa Sauce, Montana didn't eat anything.

After lunch, we all climbed back into the raft for the most exciting part of the trip. As we floated into the mouth of Santa Elena Canyon, we were in awe at the massive canyon walls that towered on both sides of us. Soon we encountered small stretches of white water rapids. I screamed with delight as the rapids hurled our raft through the rushing water. As our guide maneuvered around the boulders in our path, my confidence in his ability increased. I marveled that this man earned his living having this much fun every day! When we finally passed through all the rapids, we shed our life jackets. I lay back on the raft enjoying the tranquil float while listening to the swish of the oars through the water. All of a sudden, Montana stood up and hollered "F--- You" as loud as he could. Then he sat back down and smiled proudly as if he had conquered the canyon. Embarrassed by his behavior, I looked over at our guide for his reaction, but the expression on his face had not changed. He continued rowing as if Montana's behavior was nothing unusual. Then Montana began to ramble on in a drunken slur making absolutely no sense what-so-ever. My irritation grew as he continued this behavior for the rest of the trip. By the time we reached the end, all I wanted to do was pick up *Bessie* and head back to the campsite. However, when we arrived back at the outpost, Montana noticed the bar next door. As he headed for the door, I followed reluctantly behind. While Montana ordered himself a beer, I struck up a conversation with the man sitting next to me. With his jealousy sparked, Montana walked over to the man and threatened to shoot him if he said anything out of line to me. I couldn't believe my ears. The man looked at me in shock and asked, "Have I said something wrong?" Embarrassed, I got up and walked outside hoping Montana would follow me. I waited nervously by *Bessie* while watching the sun go down. Montana finally walked outside on the porch of the bar and hollered, "You bitch! I only wanted one more drink." Then he turned around and walked back into the bar.

I had never seen this side of Montana before. I choked back the tears as I headed across the parking lot for the outdoor rest rooms. I wasn't in there long when I heard *Bessie's* engine start up. I ran out of the bathroom yelling at Montana to stop but he continued toward me across the gravel parking lot. As I feared, he didn't make it tumbling over onto the edge of an embankment. With half the patrons of the bar now out on the front porch watching the scene, I ran over and struggled to push *Bessie's* 600 pounds off the edge of the slope. Nobody offered to help, but I couldn't blame them. No telling what Montana had said or did in the bar while I waited for him. Somehow I managed to get *Bessie* up on her two wheels, started her up and barked at Montana to climb on.

After arriving safely back at the campsite, I left Montana at the tent and headed for the campground restrooms. I broke into sobs as I realized I had a choice to make. Montana had never verbally abused me before. In fact, he had always praised and complimented me treating me with the utmost respect. Had I made a mistake bringing him with me? Would things get better or only continue to get worse? Not able to arrive at a decision about the future of *The Joyride* I headed back to the tent. A good night's sleep was what I needed.

When we awoke the next morning, Montana claimed he couldn't remember the previous night. When I reminded him how he had hollered at me, he began to apologize blaming his out of control behavior on the mixture of beer and codeine. I calmly explained to Montana how long it had taken me to save the money for *Bessie* and this trip. I added that this was a life long dream and I didn't have time to baby-sit a drunk. Montana apologized over and over reassuring me that he wouldn't drink anymore. He even joked that if he ever wanted to drink again, I should shout, "Remember Terlingua!" I wanted to believe every word he was saying, but a nagging doubt was tugging at my gut. Was he an alcoholic? As I was tossing the question around in my head, Montana promised me that if he ever did anything to upset me that he would do his best to change and correct the problem. I never had any man tell me that before. I believed him.

On our last day in Big Bend, Montana and I heard a couple of motorcycles pull in. When we saw it was the same German couple we had met back in Louisiana, we ran over to greet them. To our astonishment, the woman had not only bought and learned to ride her own motorcycle, but she had also learned to speak much better English. However, we didn't visit long because they were anxious to head to the pay showers.

Knowing how good a hot shower felt after a long day's ride, we once again said our good-byes.

After the friendships we had formed with the other campers in Big Bend, I felt a little sad when we left. But I knew there were plenty more adventures awaiting us down the road. We spent five more days touring through Texas before we headed into New Mexico. Because the nighttime temperatures kept dipping into the twenties, we decided to rent a motel room for a couple of nights upon arrival in Las Cruces, New Mexico. During our stay there, we discovered the nearby historic town of Old Mesilla that still retains much of its 1850s character. We learned that in 1858, the famous Butterfield Overland Mail and Stage Line set up its regional headquarters in Mesilla. It was there that the outlaw Billy the Kid was captured and tried. Now, Mesilla is a shopper's paradise. We had fun walking through all the shops admiring the southwestern and Indian souvenirs, clothes and silver jewelry.

I wanted to spend more time exploring New Mexico, but after learning snow covered much of the state, we headed into Arizona. We were distressed upon arriving at Chiricahua National Monument with an empty tank of gas, as there weren't any gas stations close by. Fortunately, the National Park Service allowed us to purchase two gallons of emergency gas from them. When the temperatures dipped below the freezing mark again that night, we decided that two months of camping in the cold weather had taken its toll—we were both ready for some civilization! After looking over the map, we chose Tucson for our winter headquarters. But we decided we could brave the cold a couple more nights in order to explore Chiricahua's fantasy world of rock sculptures called the *Land of the Standing-Up-Rocks* by the Chiricahua Apaches.

I got up early the next morning to pack a picnic lunch. We had to be at the Visitor's Center by 8:30 a.m. to catch the park's shuttle van that would drop us off at the top of the mountain for the nine-mile hike back through the rock formations. On the ride up the mountain, I felt caged in as I tried to view the scenery through the van's windows, I realized then just how much more I can see while riding *Bessie.*

When the park ranger dropped us off at the top of the mountain, we were immediately awed with the towering rock spires and massive stone columns. The balanced rocks that weighed hundreds of tons but were perched on small rock pedestals also impressed us. I felt like we were in a maze as we followed the trail weaving in and out among the rock formations. Along the trail, Montana discovered an opening high up in a rock wall. As he was climbing up to look inside, he stopped to ponder what he would do if an animal surprised him. I told him not to worry because I had my camera in one hand and my pepper gas in the other! Then it dawned on me that the pepper gas, which was in an aerosol can, had been through extreme temperature changes and I began to wonder if it would still work. As I held the can away from me, I hit the nozzle for just a second. It worked all right. As I watched the black cloud rise, I warned Montana to hold his breath, but my warning came too late. Upon inhaling the spray, Montana descended the rock wall coughing and gagging all the way down. I quickly apologized adding that at least we now knew the pepper gas worked!

Further down the trail, we discovered a trail register kept in a wooden box. I pulled it out to read which states other hikers had come from, but I was more intrigued by the comments that were left. Surrounded by walls of rock formations the following comments made me laugh so hard I cried:

Stoned
Let's get rocked
Mom, which tree did you use?
And to think we take it all for GRANITE!
Daughter, you ought to be ashamed of yourself!
Here a rock, there a rock, everywhere a rock, rock…
Rock of Ages, truth divine…

After my laughter subsided, I had to pause for a moment when I realized that the comments had sort of followed my life: from *stoned* to the *Rock of Ages*! Montana, who had now hiked four and a half miles in biker boots and survived a pepper gas attack, wrote his comment: "It's not the one who makes it down first who's the winner, but the one who finishes the trail at all!"

We enjoyed our picnic lunch sitting on top of a big boulder overlooking the rocky wonderland. When we felt rested enough, I took the lead down a narrow trail. My arm pushed back a branch, which then slung back with full force depositing a thorn into Montana's hand. He hollered in pain while I tried to squeeze the thorn out, but it had penetrated too deep. Montana jokingly accused me of purchasing a huge life insurance policy on him before bringing him into this maze of rocks to kill him!

I laughed harder that day than I had in a long time. I was glad that we hadn't let the cold weather discourage us from exploring Chiricahua, but we were both ready to head to Tucson where we had decided to rent a motel room with a kitchenette for a couple of months while we waited for winter to pass.

CHAPTER 8
A MARRIAGE MADE IN HEAVEN

Genesis 2:18
The Lord God said: It is not good for man to be alone,
I will make a suitable partner for him.

We arrived in Tucson, Arizona on Christmas Eve. After camping for two months in a tent, the motel room we rented with a kitchenette felt like a castle. Neither one of us had really gotten into the Christmas spirit since we had been away from home and the normal holiday activities, but I stopped at the grocery store anyway to pick up the fixings for a tasty Christmas dinner. Christmas Day we were both feeling homesick for our family and friends but Montana reassured me he was exactly where he wanted to be for Christmas—with me. Being with Montana was the best Christmas present I could have received. I had never been with a man who was so affectionate and complimentary. We both felt better, though, after we made a few phone calls home wishing our families' happy holidays. Then Montana gave me the best gift of all—he announced he was ready to marry me.

Since we didn't know anyone to marry us and I didn't want a Justice of the Peace ceremony, we didn't set a wedding date. We did take advantage of the after-Christmas sales and went shopping for our wedding rings though. Montana once again demonstrated his patience as I dragged him from one jewelry store to the next for several days looking for the perfect set of rings. While we were finding our way around Tucson, the number of homeless people we saw disturbed me. They were at almost every major intersection holding signs begging for work, money or food. Since I had experienced the pangs of hunger during my first marriage compounded by not knowing where my next meal might come from, my heart has always reached out to the hungry. We tried as often as we could to take food out to the homeless.

One day while at the laundromat, I noticed a flyer on the billboard for a New Year's Day run sponsored by the Christian Motorcyclists Association (CMA). I ripped the flyer off the board to show Montana as I excitedly explained about the CMA I had known in Florida. I suggested that maybe their chaplain could marry us. So New Year's Day we joined CMA for the group ride. What a way to start the New Year. The turn out for the ride was so large that the group was split in two. We chose the group riding to Tombstone, Arizona, known as *the town too tough to die*. It was exciting to visit the place where the famous shootout took place between Wyatt Earp, his brothers, and Doc Holliday against the Cowboy Gang. On the ride we connected with a couple named Bill and Wilma who were also getting married. Bill told us they were receiving pre-marital counseling from their pastor who was a licensed psychologist. My interest peaked when he told me his pastor also administered compatibility tests. Then Bill introduced us to the CMA chaplain nicknamed Skunk. Skunk said he would be happy to marry us as soon as he received his license which he was expecting any day.

After the ride, I suggested to Montana that since we both had failed marriages and had only been together three months, taking the compatibility test would help confirm my decision to marry him. Montana wasn't thrilled with the idea of taking a test, but when he understood how important it was to me, he agreed to participate. Since the next morning was Sunday, we visited Bill and Wilma's church. Although the pastor preached a serious message, he delivered it with such humor I felt like I was listening to a stand-up comedian. After the service we made an appointment to take the test. The test consisted of 200 questions covering all the important aspects of marriage: communication, religion, finances, family of origin issues, and role and authority issues. As I answered the test questions, I realized that we had already discussed most of them during our time around the campfires. Upon completion of the test, our answers were entered for comparison into a computer. Upon examining the printout, the pastor told us we had received one of the highest scores he'd ever seen! No doubt remained in my mind about marrying Montana. However, I wondered if Montana would still love me as much after we had been married a few years. When I expressed my concern to Montana he promised to prove his love to me by marrying me again and again every year on our anniversary!

While we waited for Skunk to get his license, we enjoyed our time in Tucson taking bike trips around the area, visiting museums, the zoo and other area attractions. We tried new restaurants, went to the movies, had cookouts with Bill and Wilma and took hikes and picnics into the desert. We also continued reading our Bible together and attending church knowing that our relationship could only survive if we were both committed to our new relationship with God that we had formed together on *The Joyride.* We were learning the difference between knowing about God to really knowing God through reading and following His Word. We took that twelve-inch journey from having God in our heads to letting him in our hearts.

Now that we were getting married, Montana felt safe to confess to me that he had been interested in me from the first day I rode my Harley into his life. After seeing me, he boasted to his friend that one day he would get me under his right arm and never let me go. For the first time Montana admitted he had fallen in love with me long before I had ever asked him to wrap one arm and one leg over me. I was shocked—what I had felt that first night we spent together was real and not my imagination!

With a mixture of surprise and delight, I declared, "You hustled me!"

"You hustled me!" he shot back. "You're the one who asked me to wrap one arm and one leg around you!"

To this day we still tease each other about who hustled whom, but we're both happy one of us did! The next Sunday, Skunk informed us at church that he had received his license and could now marry us. We rushed over to Bill and Wilma and asked if they would be our witnesses. We chose the next Friday, January 21, 1994 for an outdoor wedding at Sevenfalls, a waterfall in Sabino Canyon. Everyone liked the idea even though it meant a three-mile hike. Since I wanted our wedding night to be special, Montana and I remained celibate.

When the big day arrived, we met at church and then all of us rode our motorcycles out to the canyon. The pastor and his wife followed us out in their car so they could take pictures for us. Wilma had called ahead to the park office and found out the waterfall was dry that day, so we hiked to another spot in the canyon. Knowing we were the first couple Skunk had ever married made us feel very special. During the ceremony, Montana held me close as tears of joy welled up in his eyes while we pledged our vows. After we sealed our vows with a kiss, Skunk began to fill out our marriage license on the only thing around—a garbage can. We're probably the only couple I know who made such a special commitment legal by signing their license on top of garbage.

Following the ceremony, Montana and I celebrated with everyone over lunch at Red Lobster. Since we didn't have the traditional wedding cake, Skunk had the waiter surprise us with a dish of red raspberry cobbler topped with a lit candle. One of my favorite pictures was taken at Red Lobster of Montana and me standing under their wall menu that says *FRESH CATCH.* We held up our hands showing off our wedding rings by the sign!

After lunch, Montana and I headed back to our motel looking forward to consummating our marriage vows. We were shocked upon arrival to find such a crowd of people surrounding the motel that we could barely get in the parking lot. Policemen were attempting to direct the traffic and control the crowd. We found out what the commotion was about when we were stopped from entering our room. Three doors down they were preparing to shoot scenes for a movie with Ted Danson called *Pontiac Moon.* We could only get into our room when the film crew gave the go ahead. As we walked into our room, Montana muttered, "You can forget about being romantic tonight with all these people running around all over the place!"

I had never seen a movie production before, so we went back outside to watch the action hoping to catch a glimpse of Ted Danson. I told one of the film crew that since they were ruining our wedding night, the least they could do was get us parts as extras. The news quickly spread through the film crew and Montana grew even more irritated each time we were asked if we were the newlyweds. When we finally did see Ted Danson, we were disappointed because he looked so different from the character he had played on the television show *Cheers.*

Eventually, we tired of watching the movie production, and we went back into our room for the night. Both Montana and I had had a hard time adjusting to the dryness of the desert; so every night I boiled a pan of water to add moisture to the air. As we were lying in bed watching television, I happened to notice that our windows had steamed up from the pan of boiling water. I cracked up laughing when I realized that the crowd outside probably thought us newlyweds were inside steaming things up which couldn't have been farther from the truth! Montana could not see the humor of it all. He sarcastically suggested that we paint "Just" and "Married" on both our bottoms, pull the curtains and moon everybody.

The film crew worked until about 3:00 a.m. They had cranes with spotlights over the motel for lighting. Scenes were even shot on the roof and we could hear the actors' footsteps running across our motel room ceiling. Montana finally said, "You might as well roll over and go to sleep." So I did.

The next morning I woke up to find Montana close to tears. He explained there was no way to repeat a wedding night and he couldn't believe that I'd just rolled over and went to sleep!

"You told me to!" I defended myself. I further explained that I'd had so many things in my life not go the way I had expected that I had learned to just roll (over) with the punches. Besides, I suggested that on our first anniversary we could host a party and rent the movie so all our guests could do the same thing we did on our wedding night with us. Montana still could not find any humor in the situation, but he did give me a glimmer of hope when he said that one day he might be able to look back and laugh. We both wondered why we hadn't rented another room somewhere else!

To make matters worse, I couldn't believe that Montana had volunteered our services the next morning to clean up the church building. We went out to breakfast before we reluctantly showed up for our cleaning duties. Everyone was surprised to see us. We told them about our ill-fated wedding night. The secretary gave us a copy of our wedding vows that she had typed for me at my request. I had almost read them to the end when I came across a typing error that changed our vows to read, "Montana, you may now kill (kiss) your bride and your wife." When I showed the secretary her mistake she wanted to correct it, but we decided to leave it the way it was for a good laugh. About ten minutes later, Montana approached me with that twinkle in his eye and said, "Let's go home!" No one said a word as we rushed eagerly home to finally consummate our wedding vows!

CHAPTER 9
P.M.S. OR POST MARITAL STRESS

Romans 8:28
And we know that in all things God works for the good of those who love him who have been called according to His purpose.

Two days after we were married, Montana decided it was time for him to stop his twenty-year habit of chewing snuff. He was inspired by the fact that I had given up cigarettes, pot, and alcohol without complaint while he was still in slavery to his habits. I kept trying to tell him that I hadn't done it on my own. God had answered my prayers and taken the desire away from me.

"Well, why doesn't God deliver me?" Montana whined.

"I don't know," I replied, "why don't you ask Him?"

My kind, patient, loving husband who usually woke me up every morning with smiles, kisses and compliments, now woke up with a growl demanding his coffee! He had a difficult nicotine withdrawal and it took all the patience I could muster not to react to his irritable state. On top of our own issues, we were also worrying about Bill and Wilma. Both were very irate after their pastor had advised Bill against marrying Wilma. They were talking about quitting their church.

With all the current stress, I was looking forward to some time alone, so when Montana offered to take *Bessie* in for a tire change, I thought it was a good idea. When he kissed me good-bye, Montana told me he'd be back for lunch. However, by 3:00 p.m. Montana still hadn't returned so I called the shop where he had taken the bike. The mechanic informed me that Montana had left around noon. I called Wilma in a state of panic; but she wasn't home, so I left a message with her mother. Then I called Skunk who agreed it wasn't like Montana to just take off. Since I didn't have a phone in my motel room, Skunk agreed to call the hospitals and jails for me before coming over.

Bill, Wilma and Skunk all arrived at my motel room within minutes of each other. Bill suggested that maybe Montana was out getting drunk having sensed that mood in him the night before. Since Montana had been sober for a while that thought hadn't even crossed my mind, but I realized Bill was probably right. Knowing there was nothing we could do but wait, I thanked everyone for coming and sent them all home.

After they left, I promised God that if he brought Montana home safe, I'd never complain about him again. Not even a half hour later, Bill and Wilma returned to tell me they had found Montana in a bar right down the street. When I arrived at the bar, a scruffy looking biker approached me informing me that my husband had stormed into the bar waving his pistol while threatening to blow up the bikers' clubhouse. Being a Vietnam Veteran himself, he knew how to calm Montana down. When I asked where the gun was, the bearded man told me he had put it in the saddlebag on my bike. After thanking him for his help, I walked over to Montana who was drinking a beer at the bar. His eyes seemed to plead with me not to be angry. After giving him a hug, I asked him what happened. With slurred speech, he told me that someone had deliberately run him off the road causing him to dump the bike. He said he followed the offending car into the bar we were in which was run by an outlaw biker gang—the same bikers whose clubhouse was across the street from our motel. I didn't really believe his story; I thought he was just making excuses for getting drunk and dumping *Bessie.* I finally talked him into coming home and rode him back to the motel room. Even though I was disappointed Montana had gotten drunk, I was thankful that at least he hadn't started chewing his snuff again!

About a week later, Montana asked me to go to the store for some medicine for him. This was the first time on *The Joyride* that I had taken *Bessie* out alone. Everything went fine until on the way home. As I was sitting at a stoplight, I noticed one of the outlaw bikers getting ready to pull out of a gas station across the street. Upon seeing me, he immediately turned around and went back into the station. Instinctively, I knew he was after me. When the light turned green, I proceeded ahead. Even though he was looking the opposite direction when I passed him, it was obvious to me he was trying to act like he hadn't noticed me. I kept my eye on my rear view mirror, waiting for him to pull out after me. When he didn't I breathed a sigh of relief. Then suddenly, a white compact car appeared beside me seemingly from out of nowhere. The driver was a biker who was so big he looked like he had been stuffed into the car. He smiled flirtatiously at me, but I ignored him and sped up; then he sped up. I slowed down; then he slowed down. As I sped up again, he raced right alongside me yelling at me to pull over. After hollering back that I had nothing to say to him, I opened the throttle trying to escape his harassment. All I could concentrate on was making it back to the motel room where he would have to deal with Montana! Suddenly, the car raced ahead of me and just as I thought he was giving up pursuit, he pulled over in front of me and stopped dead in the middle of the road. When I looked behind me to see if the other lane was clear so I could pass him, the other biker from the gas station pulled up next to him. Even though they had both lanes of the road blocked, I saw that there was just enough room to squeeze *Bessie* between them. Before either one had time to react, I buzzed right through. Once again the white car took up pursuit. My heart began pounding so hard I thought I was going to stop breathing. To my relief, the car gave up the chase pulling into the biker's clubhouse.

When I finally reached our motel room, I was shaking so hard I could barely tell Montana what had happened. He grabbed his pistol saying, "Come on, we're going to straighten this out right now!" I realized what we might be facing when Montana asked me, "Are you ready to die today?" I didn't want to die, but I wasn't going to let those bikers intimidate me every time I wanted to ride up and down the road either.

We searched up and down the street, but couldn't find the man who had followed me. As we turned the bike around to head for home I suddenly saw the big guy heading in the opposite direction. I pointed at him screaming, "That's him! That's him! Turn around!" By the time we found a place to turn around, the car had disappeared. After driving up and down all the side streets, Montana decided to investigate the bikers' clubhouse. When we drove down the clubhouse's long driveway, a couple of guard dogs came running toward us.

Panicking that my legs were about to become dog food, we kept going to the end. However, no one could be found. After turning around to leave, we met a man in a pickup coming up the driveway. He pulled up alongside us. Because Montana's seat is positioned lower than mine on the bike he couldn't see that the man had a gun pointed at us. Montana asked for information about the men who had been after me. As I sat there staring down the end of that gun, Montana told the man, who turned out to be the club president, to pass on the message that he'd shoot anyone who hassled me again!

We went back to our motel room and told the manager in the office what had happened in case there was any further trouble. As we were walking back to our room, the pickup we'd just seen at the clubhouse pulled in and out stepped the man who had chased me in the white compact car. He must have been at least six feet five inches tall and all of 300 pounds. When he walked over, he looked down at me and said, "You want to step aside so we can talk to your ol' man?" He wasn't telling me where to step. I looked over at Montana for direction. When he told me to go ahead and get out of the way, I backed up.

The outlaw bikers were upset that Montana had threatened to blow up their clubhouse when he had stormed into the bar the week before after he had been run off the road. Since that incident, a couple of their own club members had been injured when someone forced them off the road. They wanted revenge. Knowing that the one biker had held a gun on us earlier, I was keeping a close eye on their hands and pockets for any sign of weapons being pulled. Even though Montana had a gun in his pocket, I had nothing for protection and felt very vulnerable out in the open. Threats were exchanged but the outlaw bikers seemed to back down when Montana reminded them that their colors (patch club members wear) didn't stop bullets. Just as it appeared the situation was calming down, out came the motel manager, looking like the character from the movie *Toy Story*, sporting a gun holster with two big guns strapped to his sides. He stood right next to Montana. I didn't know whether to be thankful or more afraid! Montana pulled a card out of his wallet which showed the club president he was a Vietnam Veteran. For whatever reason, that was enough for the outlaw bikers to make peace and shake hands. After the two men left, the motel manager explained his actions saying he didn't like the odds - two against one! As we walked back to our room Montana teased me, "Gee honey, can't you pick them any smaller?"

To combat all the stress since our wedding, we decided to do more hiking in Sabino Canyon where we had gotten married. As Montana was following behind me on the way up the trail to see the waterfalls, he made suggestive comments about my body while playfully grabbing at me. When I heard something rip, Montana exclaimed, "Look at what you did to me! I told you that you'd make me wear my pants out from the front." I turned around and couldn't believe what I saw. He had actually ripped right through the front of his pants! Even with this outrageous example of Montana's desire for me, I was still having a hard time believing that I alone was enough to satisfy Montana. In the back of my mind, I believed all men, if given the chance, would cheat on a woman, but I was learning Montana was different from the men I had known in my past. He truly seemed fulfilled with just me. In fact, he was the first man in my life who despised pornography, Strip bars, and other sexual aides. When I discussed my fears with Montana, he reassured me he didn't even entertain fantasies while making love to me. I really had a hard time believing that one because I myself was tormented with the D.T.'s (dirty thoughts). The more I wanted them to go away the worse they seemed to get. Because Montana had overcome the same problem in his past, he understood my dilemma.

Montana pointed out that these thoughts were a way of protecting myself from getting too close to him. As long as my mind was preoccupied with a fantasy during lovemaking, I was not mentally present and was missing the whole point of God's gift of becoming one with him. While listening, I had a light-bulb moment; even though I had craved an intimate relationship all my life, for the first time I realized just how terrified I was of actually being in one! Maybe that's why I had subconsciously been attracted to the emotionally unavailable men in my past!

Montana and I began praying together asking God to remove this fear. With Montana's love and patience I was finally able to clear my mind of the D.T.'s. Together we experienced the true intimacy that happens only when the physical pleasure of the sexual union is combined with the emotional and spiritual commitment to each other and God. I had, like so many others, reduced sex to just a physical act neglecting the beautiful expression of love God had originally intended it to be. Now that I had tasted the beauty of *two becoming one flesh*, which only happens in the safety of unconditional love, I finally understood a little better why God wants the sexual union limited to the marriage covenant.

After all the hiking, I was ready to get back in the wind. Montana and I headed to Salt River Canyon the following day. Along the way, Montana stopped on a deserted part of the highway so he could teach me how to shoot his gun. I really wasn't thrilled with the idea, but Montana insisted it was important for me to know how in case I ever had to use it. Montana refused to go anywhere without his gun. I was beginning to see that the Vietnam War had left more scars than Montana was willing to admit. After firing a few bullets, Montana pulled back onto the highway behind a tractor-trailer truck. When he began to pass the truck in a no passing zone leading into a curve, my worst fear became a reality when we met another tractor-trailer coming from the opposite direction. Montana let out a war hoop cry as he gunned *Bessie's* throttle and maneuvered between the two trucks. I recalled Montana's promise that if our marriage ever got boring he'd do something to spice it up. When we had safely passed through the two trucks, I leaned forward and said, "Honey, really, I'm not bored yet!"

Our final week in Tucson, we headed over to Bill and Wilma's for one last cookout. When it started to rain, Montana wanted to turn around and head back home, but I insisted that we keep going since we were already half way there. Being on an unfamiliar road, Montana slowed down when he saw railroad tracks. He was almost on top of them before he noticed the big ruts along the tracks. But it was too late. The ruts caught our tire and spun *Bessie* around like a gyroscope throwing us both off the bike. I hit the pavement so hard I bounced back up and landed on my head. Thank God I was wearing a helmet! While upside down, out of the corner of my eye, I caught a glimpse of Montana as his body rolled past me like tumbleweed. Dazed and confused I sat up. Even though *Bessie* was lying on her side facing the opposite direction than we had been heading, her engine was still running. I leaned over to try and hit the kill switch but I kept hitting her start button by mistake. The next thing I knew, Montana was picking me up out of the street to protect me from oncoming traffic. We were relieved to discover that both of us had only suffered some scrapes and bruises and the only damage we could find on *Bessie* was smashed tail pipes.

Cold, wet and stunned, we reluctantly climbed back on *Bessie* and headed for the safety and comfort of our friends. Upon arriving at Bill and Wilma's, they only had to take one look at us to know we had taken a spill. The accident had made me afraid to ride and in only a couple of days we had planned to continue *The Joyride.* When Bill and Wilma learned that our first destination was the Grand Canyon, they suggested we all go up in their van together. Since that would give me a break from the bike, I thought his suggestion sounded like a great idea. Bill loaned us his van to take home for the night. The following morning we checked out of our winter headquarters.

CHAPTER 10
STUMBLING BLOCKS INTO STEPPING STONES

Hebrews 4:16
Let us then approach the throne of grace with confidence, so that we may receive mercy and find grace to help us in our time of need.

Excitement filled the air as the four of us prepared for our trip to the Grand Canyon. It seemed like it took Bill forever to load all the camping gear into his van as I anticipated our latest adventure. Once packed, all we had left to do was stop for groceries on our way out of town. At the grocery store, I became disturbed when Bill and Montana purchased a couple cases of beer and announced they were ready to party. As soon as we were heading down the highway, Montana popped open a beer. Bill asked Montana to pass him up a beer, but I strongly objected to his drinking while driving! When Wilma began sipping from a bottle of Southern Comfort she had stashed in her purse, I wondered what I had gotten myself into. It was a sad thing to watch Bill and Wilma fall back into their old lifestyle after quitting church over the disagreement with their pastor.

By the time we reached our first camping spot near Sedona, Arizona, Montana already had a beer buzz. Bill made up for lost time by lighting up his pot pipe while Montana set up our tent. Even though it had been almost four months since I'd gotten high, I began to feel uneasy. I volunteered to cook supper to keep myself occupied. Bill passed his pipe over to Montana who then walked over to where I was cooking the hamburgers and insisted I smoke some. Montana wouldn't take no for an answer. I finally gave in to shut him up, but immediately regretted it. When I explained to Wilma how tense the pot was making me feel, she shared some of her Southern Comfort to help me relax.

After supper, we all stood around the campfire while Bill played his guitar and sang for us. As the night progressed, everyone got louder and more boisterous. Then Bill made a big mistake. Earlier, I had borrowed a pair of pants from him. When he noticed that I was wearing them he exclaimed, "Finally, I got you into my pants!" Without any forewarning, Montana smacked Bill in the chest knocking him into the bushes. More angry words were exchanged after Wilma helped Bill up. I was disgusted that the partying had turned into a drunken argument. After Bill and Wilma locked themselves in their van, Montana and I climbed into our tent. As I drifted off to sleep, I wondered if Bill and Wilma would take off without us the next day.

Upon waking up the next morning, I was really disappointed with myself for succumbing to Montana's pressure to smoke pot. When Montana finally woke up, he was also feeling ashamed. He apologized for pressuring me into smoking pot and promised it would never happen again. That was the last time I ever smoked pot. When Bill and Wilma finally stumbled out of their van, they began laughing at Montana who had run behind the tent to throw up. Bill and Wilma acted like nothing unusual had happened, so we all packed up and headed for the Grand Canyon. Montana slept most of the way. He didn't even bother to get up when we stopped for breakfast. Over breakfast, Bill and Wilma had no problem promising to keep the pot and alcohol away from us!

When we finally arrived at the Grand Canyon, we stopped at a roadside scenic overlook to gaze at the indescribable beauty surrounding us. I couldn't believe I was finally seeing this masterpiece of God's creative hand of nature. Reluctantly, we had to leave the view to find a campsite and pitch the tent. But as soon as we were situated, Montana and I hiked back to the rim of the canyon. We found a spot where we could comfortably stretch out. Montana held me close as we absorbed the stillness that flowed out of the canyon. As the sun slipped slowly over the horizon, its rays danced across the canyon walls. Somehow as we sat there, it felt like the canyon was swallowing up all our problems.

The next morning, Bill and Wilma drove us back down to the rim. I teased Montana about his hiking outfit—a pair of long johns covered by some shorts and red knee-high wool socks. We didn't have many clothes with us on *The Joyride*, so we had to make do with what we had. He looked like one of Robin Hood's merry men! Even some of the other tourists laughed and stared, but he took it all good-naturedly. At one of the lookout points, we encountered a group of Japanese students. Since Montana and I had both lived in Japan before, we remembered enough Japanese to greet them. Delighted in hearing their own language, they quickly gathered around us to have their pictures taken with us.

When we arrived at the last lookout point on the rim trail, the sound of motorcycles pulling in the parking lot stole our attention away from the canyon. To our amazement, it was the same German couple we had met in Louisiana and Texas! We learned that while we had holed up in Tucson for the winter, they had headed south and toured Mexico. Once again, they were in a hurry having heard that a snowstorm was heading our way. Sure enough, that evening while we were roasting our hot dogs over the campfire, huge snowflakes began covering the ground. As I caught a snowflake with my tongue, I wondered if our German friends had been able to ride out the storm.

The next day on our way back to Tucson, we stopped to camp at Oak Creek Canyon, which turned out to be one of my favorite spots. We pitched the tent beside a bubbling mountain stream filled with rainbow trout. Montana and I spent the afternoon trying to catch fish with only a line, hook, and bait. I didn't have any luck, but Montana, who I nicknamed *The Great White Fisherman,* caught two rainbow trout. I think our neighboring campers felt sorry for us trying to fish without a pole—they brought over six fish they had caught and gave them to us. As a joke, we told Bill and Wilma we had caught them all! We had quite a feast for dinner that night when we cooked our "catch" over the fire.

After dinner, Bill and Wilma went to bed early leaving us to enjoy the stillness of the night beside our campfire. Now that we were alone, I thought it was a good time to bring out a book I had purchased in Tucson written by Kay Arthur entitled *Lord, Where Are You When Bad Things Happen?* Montana and I had made a habit to read a little bit from it each night. This study was helping us find answers in the Bible that we had been searching for. We were learning that God could work in and through the bad things that had happened to us. But more than that, we were discovering what it means to live by faith—and rest the details of our lives in His hands. The more we focused on God's word, the more it felt like all the pieces of my life were coming together. After finishing our study that night, Montana and I snuggled by the warmth of the campfire. Marveling at the stars in the sky, we fell in love with each other all over again!

Upon arrival in Tucson the next day, we were anxious to get *Bessie* loaded up. When we went inside Wilma's house to get the rest of our gear, we caught Bill lighting up his pot pipe. Montana was furious that Bill couldn't even wait until we had left, fearing the smell of the pot smoke would tempt me. But I had no desire to even be near the stuff! As we climbed on *Bessie* to leave, my whole body stiffened with fear remembering our accident. We only went a few blocks when we both noticed a vibration coming from the front end of the bike. Feeling uneasy, we rented a motel room so we could take *Bessie* in for a checkup the next morning. It's a good thing we stopped when we did, because in the morning we discovered the problem. The accident had cracked our luggage rack, which was drooping from the weight of our pack. It was a miracle the rack hadn't snapped off causing us to dump again! Luckily, Montana found a shop next door to our motel where they welded our luggage rack securely back on. Finally, we were ready for the highway. After riding 360 miles through the Arizona desert, we arrived at Riverside State Park to camp for the night. As we fell asleep to the lonely howls of coyotes, I was thrilled to be back on the road.

Montana woke me up the next morning with a bouquet of red wild flowers in his hand suggesting we go out for breakfast.

We drove down the road until we spotted a café with white lace curtains in the window. As we were ordering our breakfast, I noticed their chalkboard menu advertising "Better than Sex Cake." An older couple sitting next to us heard me laughing at the name of the cake. They even suggested we could have our cake and eat it too! Montana replied back that he had never had a piece in public before. The jokes continued as I went up to the counter to order a piece. While out of hearing range, Montana asked the old man what they did for entertainment in such a small town. Without batting an eye, the old man replied that they swapped wives. I returned to the table with my cake. After tasting it, we both agreed that although it was delicious, the cake must have been for those who were no longer having sex! As we were leaving, the old man handed Montana one of his business cards, which Montana tossed as soon as we were outside. He wasn't interested in swapping wives!

While Montana and I put on our helmets and zipped up our leather jackets, I anticipated our next destination to Las Vegas where my sister Gay lives. As we headed down the highway, I reminisced about the trip Gay and I had taken to Europe as teenagers. So imagine my surprise when we passed through Lake Havasu, Arizona and saw the London Bridge, which had been relocated there. Twenty-three years earlier at the ages of sixteen and fourteen, Gay and I had flown to Paris to visit two exchange students my parents had hosted the year before. We paid for our trip with money earned from summer jobs. After spending a week in Paris, I realized that this was probably the only opportunity I'd ever have to see Europe. So making the most of our two weeks left, I talked Gay into hopping a train across France, crossing the English Channel by ferry and then hitch-hiking through England, Scotland and

Wales. There was nothing my exasperated parents could do when they started receiving post cards from cities other than Paris! Our impromptu trip was quite an adventure, and it was this experience that ignited my passion for traveling.

After visiting the London Bridge, we made good time as we headed for Las Vegas until we got caught in traffic due to road construction on Hoover Dam. We took advantage of the hold up to look over the dam and take some pictures. When the traffic jam lingered on for almost an hour, I began to pass the time leafing through more memories of life with my sister Gay. She came to live with my family when I was three years old. I still remember the trip our family took to a big city airport where Gay arrived directly from a Hong Kong orphanage. When I saw her for the first time, I was surprised we were the same height because she was two years older than me. As my family escorted my new sister out of the airport, I reached out to take her hand. She immediately pushed me away. Being too young to understand her fear, I remembered feeling terribly rejected.

Finally, the traffic on the dam began to move. It didn't take us too long to get to Las Vegas. I located directions to Gay's house by using the maps in a phone booth telephone book. My brother-in-law was surprised when we pulled in the driveway, commenting that most people, including UPS, got lost. I explained that after five months of traveling I could find my way most anywhere.

We spent four fun-filled days discovering Las Vegas. Gay took us on a tour of the city including the famous Strip. After stuffing ourselves at one of the great food buffets, we toured some of the more popular casinos. We allowed ourselves ten dollars worth of nickels to play the video poker games. When we beat Las Vegas out of seventy-five cents we felt lucky. Although it was fun, the realization that those grand hotels and casinos were built on people's losses saddened me.

One of the highlights of our visit to Las Vegas was visiting a church I'd heard about called Church in the Wind. The biker preacher, with waist long hair and lots of tattoos, delivered a stirring message from a podium made from the front end of a motorcycle. When I noticed that the offering plate was a gas tank from a Fat Boy Harley, I couldn't help but laugh. After church, we found out they had a similar church in Phoenix, Arizona. Everyone was so friendly, but then being bikers ourselves we fit right in. I bought a t-shirt displaying their church logo for a souvenir.

We left Las Vegas early the next morning for our 175 mile ride to Mount Zion National Park in Utah. Although we still had desert scenery on the ride over, we noticed dramatic changes as we pulled into the town of Springdale. Spring had just woken up a carpet of fresh green grass as well as the purple and white flowers on the Dogwood trees. We found our way through town to the entrance station of Mt. Zion. When the park ranger learned we were touring the United States, he sold us the Golden Eagle Pass for $25, which covers all entrance fees to any national park for a year. We wished we had learned about the pass earlier. Anxious to set up camp so we could begin exploring our new playground, we pulled into the first campground we saw. It was situated beneath a majestic mountain peak that I found even more inspiring than the Grand Canyon! After pitching the tent, we took off to climb one of the trails. As we were huffing and puffing our way up, we asked a young hiker passing us the opposite direction how far we had to go to reach the top. He replied sarcastically, "If you have to ask, you shouldn't go!" I told Montana not to feel bad because that smart aleck would be forty-four someday too! Our first sighting of a herd of Big Horn Sheep rewarded our struggle up the mountain trail.

Having our fill of hiking, we spent the following day driving the scenic route through Mt. Zion. The 1.1 mile long tunnel that was built right through the core of the mountain fascinated us. After touring the park, we drove into Springdale to browse through the tourist shops. When we noticed a restaurant's marquis advertising bumble berry pie, we were ready to try this unfamiliar dessert. However, when our bumble berry pie was served, we were disappointed to learn that it was nothing more than a pie made out of a mixture of berries, but it was still tasty.

After our visit to Mt. Zion, we headed back to Tucson to wrap up some personal business. We were both getting bored with the desert scenery and were anxious to travel on to California where we were going to meet my son Joey for his Easter break. I tried to pick the back scenic roads to Tucson to make the trip as interesting as possible. That's when I learned an important lesson: don't plan a trip with a three-year-old atlas! One of the routes I had chosen turned into a twenty-two mile stretch of gravel road, which had not been indicated on my map. To make matters worse, it was a winding steep road with long drop offs to the river below. After attempting to maneuver *Bessie* on the gravel for several miles, we were relieved to discover a National Forest Service Park. Exhausted, we immediately pulled in to camp for the night. Once again, we had a breathtaking campsite beside the water with the mountain for a scenic backdrop.

The following morning, it took us two hours to finish traveling down that gravel road. It didn't help ease our fears any when we noticed several rusted remains of cars that had plunged over the cliff's edge. However, the abundance of wildflowers along the road brightened up our spirits with their splashes of color helping to keep our minds off the gloomy prospect of death that awaited us if we slid off the side of the road.

Upon our safe arrival in Tucson, we quickly wrapped up our loose ends. Because it was late in the day, we stopped at the first state park outside of Tucson on Interstate 10, Picacho Peak State Park. That night as we sat by our campfire, we were entertained by a couple of bold kangaroo rats that darted in and out of view. We finally retired to our comfortable air mattress from which we watched the interstate below us. The hypnotic effect of the steady stream of headlights flowing down the highway appeared like watching lights run down a stream. I told Montana the interstate looked like a liquid freeway.

In the morning, we were greeted by bunches of wild yellow flowers that had popped into bloom. Montana took my picture with me sitting in the middle of the golden heaven. We had survived winter!

CHAPTER 11
OUR GOD IS AN AWESOME GOD!

Romans 1:20
For since the creation of the world God's invisible qualities—his eternal power and divine nature—have been clearly seen, being understood from what has been made, so that men are without excuse.

After two days of hard riding, we reached the California coastline. The month we spent exploring the coastline was one of my favorite parts of the trip. Ironically, the first state park we camped in, Carpinteria Beach was where we had our worst camping experience. The nightmare began when we found out the camping fees for the various California state parks ranged from $14-$23 per night. It would be impossible to stay on our budget with those prices. Then we drove into the campground and discovered that not only were the campsites right on top of one another, but also were packed with noisy campers. We finally chose one of the last spots to pitch our tent. After setting up camp, I headed to the bathroom anticipating a hot shower, only to find another disappointment—pay showers. Since I didn't have any quarters, I headed back to camp without my shower. Even though there was a bright full moon, we were too tired to stay up and enjoy the evening. We dropped into bed, hoping all the California parks weren't as noisy and crowded as this one. During the night, we were both awakened several times by trains that roared behind the campground shaking the ground as they passed. We couldn't believe these city folks called this camping! When we woke up in the morning with stiff backs due to another leaky air mattress, we couldn't wait to get out of that campground and head on up the California coastline.

We only had to travel 125 miles to find Montana de Ora State Park. This state park reaffirmed our faith in the state park system. It was named *Mountain of Gold* because of the beautiful yellow flowers found throughout the park. The park has a sandy beach as well as trails that followed the rugged mountainous coastline. The camping fee was only $7 per night because there weren't any showers, but I didn't mind since I had learned how to take baths out of a pan of water that had been heated up on the camp stove.

Early that evening, we were disappointed when a group of surfers moved into the campsite next to ours fearing they would disturb the peace and tranquility by partying into the night. To our bewilderment, they serenaded us to sleep playing a guitar and harmonica while singing praise and worship songs to God! I felt a little ashamed at having prematurely judged them. I smiled as I fell asleep listening to them sing "Our God is an Awesome God."

We spent three relaxing days in that park. We took walks along the ocean hoping to spot gray whales on their migration back to Alaska. One afternoon we watched the surfers and hand gliders while lying on the soft green grass that carpeted the cliff overlooking the ocean. Even the sea otters at play in the ocean amused us. Breathing in the fresh sea air, I felt more relaxed than I had been in months. While watching the rhythmic waves pound the beach, I realized that we had ridden *Bessie* from *sea to shining sea.*

Good Friday, we stored *Bessie* in Monterey airport's long term parking lot and transferred our gear to a rental car. After we picked up my son, Joey, we headed to Big Basin Redwood State Park. Montana and Joey got acquainted with each other while I grilled steaks, baked potatoes and corn-on-the-cob over the fire. We topped dinner off with strawberry shortcake for dessert. After dinner, we included Joey in our nightly Bible study before playing some games around the campfire.

In the morning I fixed Joey his favorite breakfast before we headed out for the three-mile trail to the waterfalls. I was amazed at the size of the giant redwoods along the trail. We learned they could grow to over 300 feet tall and live over 2000 years. As I walked along the trail admiring the redwoods, I thought of all the places I had seen that only a few months earlier had been just a dream. I felt fulfilled and emptied at the same time: fulfilled to be experiencing my dream, but emptied as I wondered what was to come next in my life. As I watched Montana and Joey running ahead of me, I thanked God for bringing Montana into my life giving me someone to build new dreams with. When we arrived at the waterfall, Joey was sure he saw a gold nugget in the water. Montana attempted to hold Joey by his ankles over the ice cold water so he could reach the nugget. Unfortunately, when Joey did reach it, he only pushed it farther away and out of sight.

Easter morning, we decided to tackle an eleven-mile trail that passed by three waterfalls. I packed a picnic before we headed out to explore the woods. Hiking the first six miles was easy, but then Montana and I began to wear out. Joey probably hiked twenty-two miles to our eleven as he kept running ahead of us and then coming back to find us senior citizens! Joey impressed us with his knowledge of the plant and animal life in the woods. We were fascinated by these slimy yellow creatures along the trail which Joey informed us were banana slugs. We found out later in our travels that Prairie Creek Redwoods State Park farther north up the coast hosts the Annual Banana Slug Derby which features events like the banana slug race, slime toss, and the banana slug joke contest! It took us seven hours to hike the eleven miles. If it hadn't been for my keen desire to see the waterfalls, I don't think I would have made it all the way. When we finally arrived back at camp, the guys built a blazing campfire. Again, we did our nightly Bible study and played some games before we all dropped into bed that night. I think we even wore Joey out.

The following morning, we let Joey choose where he wanted to spend the rest of his Spring break. He took us to a campground called the Indians in the Los Padres National Forest. Upon arrival, we were all surprised to discover that there wasn't any drinking water available. So we had to drive back to the nearest store, which was a half hour away to stock up on drinking water for the week. Since the campground had no facilities, we had to wash our dishes in the creek behind our tent. For baths we hiked to the swimming hole. One day while bathing, Joey caught a water snake. I was relieved when he let it go after playing with it for a few minutes.

After breakfast one morning, Joey asked us to join him on a hike up a rugged rocky mountainside. It took some effort for us to make it to the top, but once there we were all rewarded by the panoramic view. On the way back down, Joey was ahead of us as usual, when we heard him scream, "Rattler! Rattler!" He was so startled that he had scaled up a rock wall bruising his knee as he went. We told him to stay put until we could determine where the rattlesnake was and if there was more than one. Montana picked up some rocks and threw them ahead of us on the trail. Sure enough, we heard the distinctive sound of the warning rattles. Montana found a long stick to poke at the snake until it slithered away. As we made our way down the trail, Joey continued to throw rocks ahead of us to make sure the trail was clear.

Our week with Joey ended too soon. Before dropping Joey off at home, we stopped for a Chinese dinner and movie. Since we had to have the rental car back by 10:00 a.m. the next morning, I suggested we sleep in the car close to the airport. This way, we could return the car on time and save the money we would have spent on a motel room.

We drove back to Monterey and found a quiet street not far from the airport. Our plan of action was to put all the gear from the trunk on the front seat so we could push the back seat down making a bed for us. We unloaded the trunk as quietly as we could so as not to draw any attention to ourselves. After pushing the back seat down, I climbed in the back of our rental car, a Toyota Corolla. My legs fit through the opening to the trunk, but I was disappointed when my hips were too big to fit through. When I told Montana our idea wasn't going to work, he asked me why my hips were so big! I could only laugh at his frustration.

After putting the gear back in the trunk, Montana chose the back seat to sleep in while I climbed into the front driver seat. Unable to get comfortable, I decided to lean the seat back. However, when I pulled the lever, the seat plopped all the way back onto Montana's face. I quickly apologized as I groped for the lever to raise the seat off his head all the while trying to stifle my giggles.

We both tossed and turned finding it difficult to fall asleep in our cramped quarters.

"Montana?" I asked.

"What now?" he grumbled.

"I have to go to the bathroom," I answered.

He handed me the Gatorade bottle and impatiently asked, "Is there anything else?"

"No." I replied, "Let's try and get some sleep."

We were both finally just about asleep when my leg hit something on the dashboard setting off the emergency blinkers. Startled, I sat up and fumbled around the steering column looking for the on/off switch. When I couldn't find the switch, I resorted to the owner's manual in the glove box out of desperation. As I frantically paged through the manual, the emergency blinkers continued to flash away while Montana grumbled at me from the back seat. Finally, I found the switch to turn the blinkers off. Relieved that we hadn't aroused anyone's attention, I laughed hysterically at our situation.

When we woke up the next morning, we noticed that someone had drawn a happy face in the dew on our car window. Knowing that someone had looked in on us while we were sleeping, gave me the creeps. I decided then that I'd never again try to save money by sleeping in a car! However, we were able to return the rental car on time after dropping off all our gear at the bike. When Montana got *Bessie* loaded up, we were discouraged to discover that her battery was dead. Since airport security wouldn't give our battery a jump citing insurance reasons, we pushed Bessie out onto the road. Neither one of us had a lot of patience after our poor night's sleep in the rental car. Thankfully, we weren't on the roadside long when employees of Budget Rental Car stopped to give our battery a jump. After expressing our heartfelt thanks, we headed on our way up the California coastline.

We took our time driving up the scenic coastal highway marveling at the variety of wild flowers in bloom. We decided that we had arrived in California at the prettiest season—spring. We camped at many of the state parks that dotted the northern coastline. At one, MacKercher State Park, we spent a whole morning relaxing by the ocean while watching the harbor seals out on the rocks with our binoculars. Along came an older woman walking her dog who stopped for a few minutes to impart her knowledge about the seals. Then she began to share her life story with us including her battle to overcome alcoholism. Before she left, she commented that she believed every person you meet, even if for a brief moment, was for a purpose, that there were no accidents or coincidences. As I pondered her words, I remembered the woman we had met on top of the mountain in Alabama.

My favorite campground along coastal Highway 1 was Humboldt Redwood State Park. Even though it's the third largest state park in California exceeding 51,000 acres, as of yet the public has not discovered it. The spectacular scenic roadway that runs through the redwood groves is known as the *Avenue of the Giants*. The redwood groves stretch along thirty miles of the Eel River. We spent one day driving this scenic route, stopping at all the tourist shops along the way admiring their handcrafted redwood items from clocks to coffee tables. We also toured the *Famous One Log House* built in 1946 by Art Schmock. It took him eight months to hollow out the 2100-year-old log into a room seven feet high by thirty-two feet long. Farther along the Avenue, we toured another tree house but this one was built inside a living redwood. It was complete with electricity. We even saw a redwood tree that had a hole cut through it large enough for cars to drive through.

After spending a day driving through the redwoods, we decided to spend the next day hiking through them. We were in awe at the towering height and large circumference of these trees. Standing among these giants I could understand what inspired Joseph B. Strauss, the engineer who built the Golden Gate Bridge, to write the following poem:

THE REDWOODS

Here, sown by the Creator's hand,
In serried ranks, the Redwoods stand:
No other clime is honored so,
No other lands their glory know.

The greatest of Earth's living forms,
Tall conquerors that laugh at storms;
Their challenge still unanswered rings,
Through fifty centuries of Kings.

The nations that with them were young,
Rich empires, with their forts far-flung,
Lie buried now-their splendor gone;
But these proud monarchs still live on.

So shall they live, when ends our day,
When our crude citadels decay;
For brief the years allotted man
But infinite perennials span.

This is their temple, vaulted high,
And here we pause with reverent eye,
With silent tongue and awe-struck soul;
For here we sense life's proper goal;

To be like these, straight, true and fine,
To make our world, like theirs, a shrine;
Sink down, Oh, traveler, on your knees,
God stands before you in these trees.

As we proceeded on up the northern California coast, we stopped for lunch at the Samoa Cookhouse, which had been recommended by fellow travelers. The restaurant was formerly a cookhouse in the early 1900s for the lumberjacks working the logging and mill operations. Meals are still served, as they were then, family style with heaping bowls and platters of food along with homemade bread. Since we had both successfully quit our nicotine habits, we really enjoyed food, especially at the restaurant buffets!

When we arrived at Prairie Creek State Park, the last state park where we camped in California, we entered the visitor center. There I discovered an elk head mounted on the wall with a plaque underneath explaining this elk's fate. During the elk's mating season every fall, their behavior becomes extremely erratic when the bulls challenge for harem bull status. When the stuffed elk saw his reflection in the visitor center window, he proceeded to challenge his reflection, breaking out thirty-eight windows in the process! He stranded a ranger in the entrance station and chased visitors into a berry patch. He even challenged and damaged a visitor's car. As we drove to our campsite, I took the signs seriously that were posted along the field where the elk gathered, "Danger: Wild Animals."

Upon pulling into our campsite, we noticed a large gray metal box. I climbed off the bike and went to check it out. After pulling the heavy metal door open, I realized it would be big enough to store all of our food supplies. As Montana unloaded the bike, I read through the park brochure and discovered the reason for the metal boxes—bears. The park service had them installed after 300 bear break-ins the previous year. There was even a stiff fine for leaving any food out that might attract the bears. As we pitched our tent, I noticed the broken zipper along the bottom of the tent door. What if a bear came sniffing around? He could squeeze right into our tent. One of the neighboring campers calmed my fears when he informed us that most bears were still hibernating. Even so, we wondered as we snuggled in our tent that night, if we'd have any surprise visitors.

CHAPTER 12
SEARCHING FOR HOME

Jeremiah 29:11
"For I know the plans I have for you," declares the Lord,
"plans to prosper you and not to harm you,
plans to give you a hope and a future."

Leaving California behind, we headed up through Oregon on Interstate 5. We chose that route instead of the scenic coastal highway so that we could explore the cities in Oregon for a possible place to make a new home. Ever since we had purchased our first piece of furniture in California, a redwood coffee table, I began to long for a home to put it in! We had both come to the conclusion during *The Joyride* that Daytona Beach was not a good place for us to return to until we had conquered our addictions. So we hoped to discover our new home while traveling through the west.

We spent the first night in Oregon camped in Stanton County Park. We pitched our tent across from five RV's whose occupants were sharing a potluck supper. Being the end of April, the campgrounds were getting more crowded and Montana and I discussed the fact that by the summer they would only be more so. Worn out from our ride, we went to bed early that night without even making a fire.

In the morning, the people across the way watched curiously as we loaded all our gear on *Bessie*. One man finally came over to express his amazement that we had gotten it all on! We learned that the five couples had been friends for forty to fifty years ever since they had met in church. One of the gentlemen in the group had been their pastor. I was impressed that not only had their marriages survived, but they had all maintained their friendships for so many years as well. As the five couples were saying their goodbyes to each other, they formed in a circle for prayer. Montana hollered over to them to wait for us as we ran over and joined them.

That morning, we headed for Silver Falls State Park near Salem, Oregon. On the way we saw acres of rolling hills of lush green grass. We wondered why crops weren't planted instead until we saw the sign at a farm advertising their grass seed that was shipped all over the world. It was interesting to see the fields of Christmas trees being grown for future holidays as well as the fields of grape vineyards. We were driving through the Wilamette Valley where thousands of people had arrived from the east on the Oregon Trail in hopes of a new life in the 1800s. I smiled as I thought of us as the modern pioneers searching out west for a new life.

After arriving in Silver Falls State Park, we learned the park had a trail which passed ten waterfalls. The next morning we set out with a picnic lunch to find them. We were amazed at the beauty and variety of the waterfalls. I was falling in love with Oregon and was especially impressed with the friendliness of the people.

The following day, we drove through Portland on our way to Ainsworth State Park situated along the scenic Columbia

River Gorge. The Columbia River Gorge is famous for its waterfalls including seventy-seven on the Oregon side alone. We drove scenic Highway 30 to observe some of them including Multnomah Falls, which plunges an amazing 620 feet. While on the scenic drive, we talked to various people we met about living in Portland. We also looked through the phone book for companies we could find employment with. In addition, we bought a newspaper to find out about prices for renting homes, food and other general information. We had followed this same procedure in other cities that we were interested in as possible future homes.

From Oregon, we drove to Seattle where we camped in a private campground. We spent two days getting familiar with that area. Although we found Washington very beautiful, we both agreed that Oregon remained as our first choice. But Montana had always dreamed of moving to Denver, Colorado so we decided to head their next.

Our ride the next day took us through some diverse scenery from snow packed mountains down into forested hills on down to desert like terrain. After 408 miles, we arrived at Farewell Bend State Park near the eastern Oregon State line. Since we had ridden so many miles in one day, we spent the next day relaxing in the park. We walked down to the Snake River where we fed some wild ducks. I got a kick out of watching the gophers pop in and out of their holes along the river. When we found out from the park ranger that the Oregon Trail was nearby, we set out to find the historical road.

Although all that can be seen of the Oregon Trail is big ruts, I realized it was more than just an old dirt road. The trail symbolized a growing nation on the move. As I walked along the ruts, I tried to imagine the creak of the worn out wagon wheels as men, women and children wearily pushed forward. We learned that nearly 350,000 emigrants followed this trail to the west beginning in the 1840s. How difficult their journey must have been without the modern roadside conveniences Montana and I enjoyed on *The Joyride.*

After traveling 340 miles the next day, we checked into a motel room in Tremonton, Utah. When we heard that a snowstorm had just hit Denver, we decided to head into southern Utah for a few days while the snow melted. We made it all the way to Bryce Canyon National Park the following day. After the spring weather we had been enjoying, we were surprised when the temperature dropped down to twenty degrees that night. We were even more surprised when we woke up the next morning, Montana's birthday, to a snowstorm. We huddled in the tent as we watched the snowfall amazed by the accompanying thunder and lightning. I sang "Happy Birthday" to Montana while substituting an Oreo Cookie for a birthday cake and a cigarette lighter for a birthday candle. Montana remarked that this was the first birthday he had ever spent stranded in a tent on top of a mountain watching a snowstorm!

When the sun rose the next morning, it quickly melted the snow off the roads. We decided we'd better head out while we had the chance. We followed Route 12 through southern Utah, which rewarded us with spectacular scenic views. Because there was absolutely no vegetation in some places around the wind carved rocky cliffs, I told Montana it looked like we were riding on another planet!

Along Route 12, we met another couple from California who were riding their Harley to a rally in New Mexico. When they found out that we'd been on the road for seven months, they had all kinds of questions for us. They were especially amazed by how much gear we had loaded on the bike. The man informed us that he owned a Harley dealership before pointing out that the luggage racks were only intended to carry about ten pounds. Since we had a hundred pounds loaded on ours, I commented that our guardian angels must have been protecting us! The man remarked that we were doing what so many bikers had only dreamed of doing! He handed me his card and told me to contact him when I finished the book I had told him I would be writing about *The Joyride.*

Further along Route 12 at a gas station, we met a group of ten bikers who were also heading to the rally in New Mexico. But I didn't find them as friendly as the couple we had just met. As I waited for Montana to pay for our gas, I noticed a woman sitting on a Harley with a man standing next to her. I asked her if they took turns driving like Montana and me. She replied in the most snobbish voice, "Oh no! We each have our own bikes." Nobody in the group seemed to want to make conversation. I stood awkwardly waiting for Montana to come out of the store.

When we arrived in Green River, Utah, we stopped again for gas. As we pulled in the station among another group of bikers, a man sarcastically commented, "Do you think you have enough stuff loaded on your bike?"

I had had enough of this Harley snobbery so I shot back, "I think so considering we've been on the road for seven months." Then inside the station a woman who was standing next to me while I paid for my gas bragged, "Me and my old man just rode 8,000 miles!"

"Well, that's nothing," I shot back, "We just did 14,000!" We were taken aback by the snobbish attitude of the bikers we had encountered, which was so different from the bikers we had known in Florida.

During breakfast the next morning, our waitress told us about Crystal Geyser. Since we'd never seen a geyser before, we decided to try and find it. Our waitress warned us that the geyser only went off three or four times a day at irregular intervals since vandals had dropped dynamite down the opening. She added that her daughter had to wait six hours before the seventy-five foot spray of water rewarded her. We decided to take our chances hoping we wouldn't have to wait that long.

As we set out on the ten-mile gravel road to find the geyser, we almost changed our minds and turned around. The road was one of the most treacherous routes we had taken *Bessie* on. Montana had to travel slowly to maneuver between the large rocks and ruts taking us almost an hour to reach our destination. The geyser was located beside a river and surrounded by flat rock. After looking down the geyser's opening, we found a place to relax while waiting for the water show. Every once and a while the geyser would begin to bubble and boil up about two feet exciting our anticipation of the seventy-five foot spray of water. After waiting patiently for two hours, we began to get bored. I figured if the geyser wasn't going to go off at least we could! Montana was delighted by the surprise ending to our excursion before we headed back to our motel room.

The next morning as Montana was loading up *Bessie* for our ride; a bungee cord snapped loose hitting him so hard on the forehead it knocked him down. I was just thankful it had missed his eye! After regaining his composure, we were soon loaded up and heading down the highway. When Montana spotted a golden eagle sitting proudly in a field with two antelope nearby, he excitedly proclaimed that we were getting closer to home. After riding ninety more miles, we reached the Colorado State line where we found the Visitor's Center. Inside we found so many brochures on the state it was hard to decide which ones to keep. The hostess informed us that the Colorado National Monument was nearby, so we camped there for the night so we could plan our attack on Colorado.

The campground was perched on top of the mountain overlooking the valley. We pitched our tent facing the spectacular view. After reading through the brochures, Colorado sounded like a fun state to explore, but we weren't sure what areas were accessible by motorcycle due to the snow. After some discussion we decided to just head straight to Denver. If we liked Denver, we agreed to return to Florida to get our belongings and end *The Joyride* four months early. Although I still wanted to tour Montana, Wyoming and Alaska, it would be at least another month before those states would be accessible by motorcycle. We reasoned that if we moved to Denver we would be close enough to tour those states later. I didn't realize it then but the Colorado National Monument was the last place we were to camp.

The next morning we drove 260 miles across the Rocky Mountains to Denver. There was still snow on the mountains; even some of the ski resorts were still in operation. Upon arriving in Denver, we rented a motel room. As Montana unloaded the bike, I studied the phone book maps familiarizing myself with the layout of Denver. We spent the next five days learning our way around the city. Since the construction industry was booming, Montana discovered he'd have no trouble finding a job. We found an apartment we really liked, but the manager didn't have an opening until July. So we left her a deposit to add our name to her waiting list.

I felt more stress those five days in Denver than I had experienced during the past seven months. Although we were both ready to settle down, the decision to stop *The Joyride* early was a difficult one. And settling down in a city of two million people hadn't exactly been what I had envisioned for my new home. I like small towns. I knew *The Joyride* was probably the only opportunity in my life until my retirement that I would be able to travel as freely as this. I wanted to be sure I didn't regret my decision later. Finally the stress built up in both of us until we had the worst argument of our marriage. In anger, Montana left me at the motel room. When he hadn't returned in several hours, I called my best friend back in Florida crying my heart out. As usual, she had a calming effect on me reassuring me everything would work itself out. Montana finally returned around 11:00 p.m. with a police escort. After the police checked his driver's license and registration, I was astonished that they let him go, as he was obviously drunk. We both went to bed without saying a word to each other.

We packed up in silence the next morning. As we headed out Interstate 70 toward Kansas, I felt miserable about our fight. Not able to stuff my feelings any longer, I began to sob as the pain and frustration spilled out. Montana pulled over so we could talk. Montana shared that he felt something was missing in his relationship with God because no matter how much he read the Bible or prayed he just couldn't seem to live the way he thought he should. And when he didn't drink for a while, painful memories were coming back to haunt him. "Wasn't life supposed to get easier when you became a Christian?" he wondered out loud. I didn't have any answers. I was wrestling with my own emotions. Every time Montana went off and got drunk I felt abandoned. I was beginning to wonder if our marriage would survive. We both agreed that when we settled down we'd seek some counseling. Feeling reassured that Montana was willing to do anything to protect our marriage; we climbed back on *Bessie* and headed down the road. Our spirits picked up as we drove past fields upon fields of golden wheat, which filled the air with a fresh sweet smell. We rode as far as Salina, Kansas where we rented a motel room for the night. I called my childhood friend in Springfield, Illinois to alert her to our arrival the next day.

We made it all the way to Springfield by the following evening. After riding 940 miles in two days on the back of *Bessie* I thought my bottom side would never feel the same! We spent the next five days visiting friends there. Although I had grown up in Springfield, it didn't feel like home anymore. I had to laugh when I realized I really didn't have a home anywhere!

After our visit to Springfield, we headed back to Florida. Anxious to get back home, we drove as far as we could each day. On the second day back, we passed a black woman in Tennessee who had pulled over on the side of the road. When she saw us pass by, she waved frantically to get our attention. I noticed that she was crying hysterically. As our eyes met but for a second, I felt her pain. I urged Montana to go back and find out what her problem was. By the time we had turned around on the shoulder, we noticed another man had stopped to help. When we pulled up she explained that her car had overheated. She left us standing there while she went back to the man's car to call for help on his cellular phone. She was so upset that she carelessly left her purse behind on the front seat of her car. We waited for her to return wondering what we could do to help. When she walked back, she shocked us by telling us that Jesus had told her to flag us down! I wanted to stay with her until help arrived because she seemed so vulnerable sitting alone along the highway. Even though she insisted she'd be all right, I flagged down a passing state trooper feeling relieved when he responded. She wanted to know if she owed us any money. Montana asked her to just keep us in her prayers. As we headed back down the highway, Montana chuckled as he explained that she must have powerful prayer—three different vehicles had stopped to offer her assistance. He added that he hoped she would pray for us!

The last day all the way back to Florida my stomach was tied up in knots. We were about to return to where we had started. Every time Montana and I stopped for a break, he would say to me, "You don't have anything to worry about when we get to Florida. I'm not going to get drunk."

The last time he said that to me, I replied, "Who are you trying to convince? Me or yourself?"

When we finally arrived at our old hangout, our friends ran out and greeted us with shrieks and hugs. Dinner was cooking on the grill and the party began! The usual crowd stopped in and out all night—it was just like it was when we left. Having learned my lesson on our Grand Canyon trip, I managed to have fun even though everyone was drinking, including Montana. When Montana started the next day with a beer, I decided to go stay with a girlfriend. I told Montana to come pick me up when he was done partying. All Montana heard me say was that I was leaving him. He insisted that I stay with him. I finally had to admit to myself that I wasn't upset because I felt tempted by all the partying, but I was upset because I couldn't control Montana's drinking—and I wanted him to stop. I had to accept the fact that although we had both begun a walk with Jesus, we had each started from different points. Just because God had brought me to a place where I could say no to alcohol and pot, didn't mean Montana should be at the same place. Accepting my powerlessness over Montana's drinking, I turned the situation over to God. There was no denial now that Montana truly needed an inner healing from his past before he was going to find any peace. Knowing what a long hard road it had already been for my own healing, I knew there was going to be some difficult times ahead for us. But I really loved Montana and was committed to stand by him through the process. Three days later, Montana announced he'd had enough of drinking.

The following morning we received a phone call from the apartment manager in Denver with the news that she had an apartment ready for us in ten days! We spent the rest of our time in Florida with Montana's parents trying to fit in all our visits with my daughter and friends before leaving one more time.

CHAPTER 13
THE RIDE CALLED LIFE

Philippians 1:6
Being confident of this, that he who began a good work in you will carry it on to completion until the day of Christ Jesus.

Sunday morning we left Daytona Beach in our car pulling *Bessie* behind us on a trailer. All we brought with us were our clothes and a few sentimental keepsakes. After three days on the road, we arrived in Denver hot and tired. As we signed a myriad of papers to lease our new apartment, I felt a touch of sadness that *The Joyride* was over. However, when we were handed the keys to our first home together, my enthusiasm returned. After climbing three flights of stairs to our apartment, I asked Montana if he would carry me across the threshold—no easy task since I had gained fifteen pounds on *The Joyride.* Montana took a deep breath before picking me up. While wrapping my arms around him, we kissed as we stumbled through the doorway. We were home!

Feeling lost in our empty apartment, we spent the next couple of weeks shopping for everything we needed to make us feel at home. It didn't take us long to learn our way around the area as we shopped from one store to the next spending all the money left over from *The Joyride.* Exhausted after each day's shopping spree, we relaxed in our apartment complex's pool and hot tub.

Once we were rested and settled in our new home, we both began job hunting. I was impressed when after only one phone call Montana found a job as a foreman of a plastering crew for a local construction company. I became discouraged though, when I realized it wasn't going to be as easy to find a job in my field as a Medical Technologist. Even though Montana told me to take my time, I had difficulty adjusting to my days without him. After all, we had just spent our first eight months together without being separated.

All my life I had wondered what it would be like to be a housewife with someone else supporting me for a change! Since I finally had the opportunity, I took advantage of my leisurely days until I could find a job. I began writing this book about *The Joyride* wondering if my story would be interesting enough to land me on my favorite talk show.

Montana also had a hard time adjusting to his days back in the workforce. Not only was he physically out of shape, but also he was mentally unprepared to deal with the other two foremen who had a habit of drinking beer on the job. Since they worked on scaffolding several stories high, Montana worried about everyone's safety. But the real pressure came from the temptation of being around the beer. When Montana tried to discuss the problem with his boss, he was told to look the other way because the company didn't have enough plasterers to fire anybody! That's when Montana said he should have quit the company, but knowing he was our sole source of income he confronted the two foremen instead. The confrontation turned into a heated argument with crewmembers taking sides. Fortunately, there were enough crewmembers that felt the same way as Montana, but had not had the courage to take a stand. These men became Montana's new crew.

One Friday afternoon, these two foremen showed up on the job site with everyone's paychecks and a cooler full of beer. Although they were not assigned to work at that site, they continued to hang around drinking beer until the end of the workday. Since they weren't working, Montana ignored them concentrating on finishing up his work before the weekend. When Montana got home from work that night, he received a phone call from his boss informing him that a hot tub was missing from his job site. Immediately Montana called members of his crew for information. One of them had witnessed the foremen unhooking the hot tub. Montana called his boss with the information. A few days later, the foremen confessed to the crime and were arrested. In retaliation, they implicated Montana as a partner in the crime. When the detective continued to question Montana and his crewmembers we decided it was time to consult a lawyer. We'd only been in Denver a month and already it felt like our world was being turned upside down.

Even though Montana and I had visited different churches, we still had not found a church home and I began to feel isolated and lonely in the big city. Remembering the friends I had made through the CMA in Florida and again in Arizona, I began to search for a CMA chapter in Denver. After calling several churches without any success, I became frustrated. However, when I bought tickets for a July 4th Family Festival at Bandimere Speedway, I learned that Christians owned it. I had a feeling I might find the CMA thru them.

On July 4th, we headed for the speedway. Even though we arrived early, a line of cars had already formed. Suffocating from the sweltering July heat, I got out of our car and struck up a conversation with the woman in the car next to us. It just so happened that her father was a member of CMA. Through him, we met with both chapters in Denver. We began to form new friendships as we attended the club meetings and group rides. I felt connected again.

Just when things appeared to be improving, we received two disturbing phone calls. The first was Montana's mother informing us that his father had passed away. The second call came from our lawyer informing us that Montana was being charged in the missing hot tub case with two felony counts: theft and conspiracy of theft! In shock, I drove to Montana's job site to break the news. After gathering his tools, we headed to his office to find out if his company would help pay our legal fees to prove Montana's innocence. When they refused, Montana walked off his job. Now, not only was Montana facing criminal charges, we didn't even have an income! Why did the saying, "Life is what happens when we've made other plans!" always seem to demonstrate itself in my life? It wasn't easy not worrying, but I held on to God's promises in the Bible to take care of us. Although I didn't understand why all this was happening to us, I knew I now had an opportunity to exercise my faith I had acquired on *The Joyride.* I would have to have patience while I waited to see how God was going to work this all out for our good! I really admired Montana when he went out the next day and found a new job. Each morning before work he got up an hour earlier than necessary so he could read his Bible and spend time with the Lord. I knew it was only a matter of time before God made Montana whole, healing up the wounds from his past.

When we called our new friends in the CMA with our problem, we received a lot of support. Not only did they listen sympathetically, but they also kept us uplifted in their prayers. Several members even stopped by our home to see if there was anything else they could do for us. The whole situation just seemed so unfair to me. Montana had gotten away with so many crimes in the past, but now that he had surrendered his life to follow Christ why was he being charged with a crime he hadn't even committed?

One afternoon while Montana was napping, I turned to my Bible for comfort. Reading Psalm 37 gave me courage to face the new challenges in our life. When I realized that I was turning to God's Word for relief instead of cigarettes, pot or alcohol, I knew *The Joyride* had been a success.

The Joyride, which had lasted eight months covering 19,000 miles through twenty-three states, had turned out to be everything I had dreamed it would be. As I drifted off into fond memories of my trip, I knew that even though T*he Joyride* was over, God would continue to be with us on the rest of our adventurous and unpredictable ride called life.

POSTSCRIPT

So whatever happened to Montana? The legal proceedings for the felony theft charges stretched out over a five-month period. Emotionally and financially drained, Montana accepted a plea bargain, even though he was innocent, just to end the legal fight. However, all the stress drove Montana to seek counseling from the Vets Center in Denver where he was diagnosed with Post Traumatic Stress Disorder (PTSD) resulting from his Vietnam War tours of duty. After moving back to Florida in February 1995, Montana had a nervous breakdown, (or what Joy calls a spiritual breakthrough!) and checked himself into the Gainesville Veterans Hospital where he finally faced his painful past and learned to recognize his PTSD symptoms. He has never had another drink since.

Upon his discharge, Joy introduced Montana to a Christian twelve-step program. Through continued study of God's Word, with support of Christian brothers, and with the power of the Holy Spirit working in his life, Montana found the hope and healing he had been searching for. In 1997, Montana and Joy settled down in the small community of Lake Helen, Florida. Montana has kept his promise to Joy: each year they renew their wedding vows on their anniversary thankful that not only have they survived another year together, but they are still passionately in love! Both continued their walk with the Lord, answering God's call to serve His Kingdom in full-time ministry.

Currently, Montana and Joy are ordained Pastors serving at Living Water Free Methodist Church in Orange City, Florida. Their hearts desire is to help others find this freedom thru the preaching and teaching of the Word of God. They may be contacted at montanajoy@embarqmail.com.

DISCUSSION GUIDE

CHAPTER ONE: LET YOUR DREAMS TAKE FLIGHT

1. Do you have a dream? Do you think it's possible to make your dreams come true? What steps have you taken to realize your dreams?

2. Do you talk about your dreams with others? If so, what kind of reactions do you get? How would you handle someone who discourages your dream?

3. Like the author who battled loneliness, what struggles do you face in your day-to-day life? Do you think you handle these challenges in healthy or unhealthy ways?

4. What role does God, the Creator of heaven and earth, play in your life? Does He seem distant and unavailable or close and concerned? Read Psalm 34:18.

5. Does having courage to follow your dreams mean you will never feel fear?

CHAPTER TWO: THE SURPISE BEGINNING!

6. Would you ever attempt to take a yearlong trip anywhere alone? Why or why not?

7. How do you make life-altering decisions? Who do you go to for counsel or advice?

8. Like the author, have you ever made a promise to yourself not to do something and then didn't keep it?

9. Do you think it's possible to fall in love with someone in ten days? What did you think of this surprise beginning?

10. Have you ever read the Bible? Do you think it has any relevance for your life today? Read Psalm 37:4.

CHAPTER THREE: GOOD-BYE MEANS HELLO

11. What people in your life would you have a hard time telling good-bye to for a year?

12. What do you do when your loved ones make choices that you disagree with or hurt you?

13. What did you think of the author's parents requiring separate bedrooms?

14. Are you able to let go of the familiar to discover the unknown? Have you ever felt free? Read Isaiah 40:31.

CHAPTER FOUR: WHICH STATE WILL BE BEST?

15. Do you give up when plans don't turn out the way you expected?

16. Have you ever tried to live your life without television, cell phones, and computers? How do you think this would affect your relationships?

17. Why was the author studying the Bible every night? Read Psalm 119:105.

18. Do you believe that each person you meet has a purpose in your life?

CHAPTER FIVE: TRUST

19. Have you ever felt lost? Have you ever wondered why you are here?

20. Do you blame others for your problems? Do you blame God? What does it mean to take responsibility for our lives?

21. Do you have a hard time trusting others?

22. Can you see that the author met two types of people on *The Joyride*? One group pointed her to trust in God; the other group pointed her away from God and back to the lifestyle she was trying to escape. Can you see that pattern in your life?

23. Do you think God is good? Read Psalm 34:8.

CHAPTER SIX: DON'T MESS WITH TEXAS

24. Do you have any prejudices?

25. When you meet people, do you listen to your gut reaction or heed the red flags? Why do you think denial is such a powerful force in our lives?

26. Which one does forgiveness set free…the victim or the offender? Do you have anyone in your life you need to forgive? What will happen to the offender?

27. Have you ever done anything out of desperation, only to regret it later? What did you learn from that experience?

28. Why is it so important who we choose to let in our lives? Read 1 Corinthians 15:33.

CHAPTER SEVEN: COYOTES, ROAD RUNNERS, JAVENLINAS OH MY!

29. Has anyone's behavior ever embarrassed you?

30. When in a crisis and emotionally upset, is that a good time to make decisions?

31. Can you reason with someone under the influence of alcohol or drugs?

32. Why is it so important to have fun and laugh? Have you ever seen parallels in your life like the author did when she read the comments in the trail register?

33. Do you think maybe the Divine orchestrates coincidences? Read Psalm 46:10.

CHAPTER EIGHT: A MARRIAGE MADE IN HEAVEN

34. Do you think God can choose your mate or do we choose our mate? Read Genesis 2:18.

35. Do you think pre-marital counseling helps a marriage be better? Why or why not?

36. Do you think it's possible to be in love with someone for a lifetime? Is love just a feeling? Why do you think there are so many divorces?

37. What is the difference between knowing about someone and really knowing them? Do you know about God or do you really know Him?

CHAPTER NINE: P.M.S. OR POST MARITAL STRESS

38. What is it about the marriage vows that allow us to relax and be ourselves?

39. Can you control a person and their choices? When another person's choices affect you negatively, what can you control? Read Romans 8:28.

40. Are you afraid of intimacy? Do you see sex as more than just a physical act? Do you realize that God created you as one person with three parts: spirit, soul and body?

41. Do you struggle with the D.T.'s? Are you able to share anything with your mate? Have you ever prayed together?

CHAPTER TEN: STUMBLING BLOCKS INTO STEPPING STONES

42. Have you ever had someone close to you pressure you into doing something you didn't want to do? Why do you think this happens?

43. Have you ever gotten sick and tired of being sick and tired? When does lasting change take place? Read Hebrews 4:16.

44. Has anyone ever shown you mercy? What is grace and how does it help us?

CHAPTER ELEVEN: OUR GOD IS AN AWESOME GOD!

45. Can you find humor in frustrating circumstances?

46. Have you ever prejudged someone only to discover they were not what you thought? Have you ever had anyone misjudge your character? How did it make you feel?

47. Why does spending time in nature at places like the Grand Canyon and the Redwood forests move us so deeply? Read Romans 1:20.

CHAPTER TWELVE: SEARCHING FOR HOME

48. Do you like where you live? Do you think relocating will make you happier?

49. Like the five couples the author met, have you ever met a group of people who had what you wanted? What stood out about their life?

50. Do you think our life today is much different from generations past? In what ways is it the same? In what ways is it different?

51. Do you believe God has a plan for your life? Read Jeremiah 29:11.

CHAPTER THIRTEEN: THE RIDE CALLED LIFE

52. How did you feel when the decision was made to end *The Joyride* early?

53. Did moving to Denver make Montana's life any easier? Why or why not?

54. Have you ever been accused of something you did not do? Is life always fair?

55. What changed in the author's life that enabled her to stand firm through the trial?

56. Before you read the postscript, did you have confidence that Montana would get set free from his past and live a victorious life? Read Philippians 1:6.

57. Are you ready to accept God's free gift of salvation, Jesus Christ, and have an exciting and adventurous ride through life?

Please feel free to contact the author at
montanajoy@embarqmail.com

TO THE READER

No matter where you are and no matter where you've been, you have not gone too far or done too much that the love of Jesus can't forgive!

Jesus loves you so much that he gave His life for you so that you could not only be with Him forever in eternity but also have an exciting life here on earth full of love, peace and joy. Psalm 37: 4 says *Delight yourself in the Lord and he will give you the desires of your heart.* You don't have to do anything or change anything to earn God's love; it's a free gift that was paid for by Jesus' sacrifice. When you receive this free gift, the Holy Spirit will come into your heart; teaching, guiding and comforting you on your ride through life until Jesus returns to take you home.

Go to Him now and tell Him what's on your heart. Ask Him to lead you to a group of believers that can help you learn and grow in the Lord.

And read your Bible: God's love letter to you. It says in Romans 10:9 *That if you confess with your mouth, "Jesus is Lord" and believe in your heart that God raised him from the dead, you will be saved.*

May the Spirit of God set you FREE!

ABOUT THE AUTHOR

Joy F. Mormur graduated with honors from University of Illinois-Springfield in 1985 with a B.S. in Medical Technology. She worked twenty years as a Medical Technologist in various hospitals and private laboratories analyzing blood and other body fluids, which aids the physicians in diagnosing and monitoring treatment of disease. In 1992, Joy participated on a Catholic Medical Mission, along with forty other medical professionals, to the Dominican Republic. Along with two others, she secured donated supplies and equipment to help set up a laboratory there.

In November 2000 Joy and her husband Montana began a church-planting project for the Free Methodist Church. Following her passion and calling, Joy became an ordained Pastor with the Free Methodist Church. Joy and her husband now serve as Co-pastors at Living Water Free Methodist Church in Orange City, Florida where Joy has started a community service called *The P.I.T. Stop for People In Transition*, which offers showers, use of a washer and dryer, and meals to the homeless. Ten percent of the profits from this book will be donated to this community service and other projects to aid the homeless.

Joy is a popular speaker to women's groups. She has spoken in various churches throughout Florida and at women's retreats.

Joy and Montana have four children and nine grandchildren. They also support two children through International Child Care Ministries: one in Haiti, and one in Burundi.

Along with all the other children and grandchildren who have adopted them through their ministry; the author says her family is constantly growing!

Intermedia Publishing Group

Publishing That Works For You

Do you need a speaker?

Do you want Joy Mormur to speak to your group or event? Then contact Larry Davis at: (623) 337-8710 or email: ldavis@intermediapr.com or use the contact form at: www.intermediapr.com.

Whether you want to purchase bulk copies of *The Joyride* or buy another book for a friend, get it now at: www.imprbooks.com.

If you have a book that you would like to publish, contact Terry Whalin, Publisher, at Intermedia Publishing Group, (623) 337-8710 or email: twhalin@intermediapub.com or use the contact form at: www.intermediapub.com.